CW00543091

ASTROLOGY OF THE 13 SIGNS OF THE ZODIAC

Klaudios Ptolemaios Publications

Klaudios Ptolemaios Ltd
Plovdiv 2012
info@klaudiosptolemaios.com

ISBN 978-954-92725-1-2

2nd Edition revised: April 2012

Cover: "Planets"
by Maria Kanata

Vasilis A. Kanatas

ASTROLOGY OF THE 13 SIGNS OF THE ZODIAC

Ophiuchus: The New Sign of the Zodiac Circle

Klaudios Ptolemaios Publications

Contents

Prologue

A physicist with an interest in Astronomy may notice objects in the night sky not easily "visible" to the average person. Almost every time he observes the maps of the skies, he finds the horoscopes of Western Astrology amusing because they almost always place the planets in the wrong positions. On March 14th 2011, for example, the planet Mars is placed in the Constellation of Pisces, when it is actually in Aquarius. I know this well as a physicist and amateur astronomer because at night I can scan the starry sky and see for myself that the planet Mars (on March 14th 2011) is in Aquarius, contrary to the convictions of Western Astrology.

The same inaccuracy with regard to position applies not only to the other planets of our solar system, but also to the Sun and the Moon. By extension then, the constellations of the zodiac are also in positions different from those assigned to them by Western Astrology, and indeed a new zodiac constellation, Ophiuchus, has been identified in the path of the Sun on the ecliptic.

I used to be firmly opposed to Astrology, mainly because it annoyed me that everything it had to say was outdated; it used a faulty coordinate system and, most of all, it ran completely contrary to science. Astronomy, which should be the basic reference point for Astrology, has been forgotten by Western Astrologers and the subject matter of their work has tended to become a new religion.

In this book, we will create new foundations for Astrology using the discoveries of Astronomy, and examine some interesting new astrological concepts. For example, of particular interest is Percy Seymour's theory regarding the influence of the planets on our lives, and this is developed in brief in the first chapter of the second part of the book. We will also take a look at the circle of the zodiac, putting aside our reservations and preconceived ideas. We will see that it is possible to put astrological prediction on a new footing. We will look at the truth of the New Zodiac.

Certainly most of you will have seen the predictions of traditional Astrology fall short. Most of them will say ten different things in order to get one right. You are not as they describe you, for the simple reason that they are using the wrong zodiac sign, the wrong planets and the wrong ascendant. Try it and you will see how different and how much closer to the truth the Astrology of the 13 Signs of the Zodiac is. At last, you will discover your true zodiac sign and your real horoscope. Above all, you will realize that your zodiac sign is demonstrably the right one based on scientific interpretation.

Follow us into a new scientific approach. On our journey we will attempt to give Astrology a firm foundation in Astronomy, and to redefine its much misunderstood principles.

Vasilis A. Kanatas

Introduction

Astrology has been tightly bound to Astronomy since ancient times. Many ancient peoples were concerned with these sciences, but the Greeks were the first to organize, systematize and reveal them.

One could argue that the talent of the ancient Greeks lay precisely in their ability to create the foundations and to systematize knowledge to the extent that it could withstand the passing of the centuries, and today almost everyone would accept these discoveries as theirs. So, our ancient ancestors invented or systematized heroic epic poetry, sport and the Olympic Games, theater, democracy, mathematics, geography, Astronomy, rhetoric, philosophy and many other disciplines and ideas.

It is not surprising then that, in the 2nd century B.C. in Hellenistic Alexandria on the continent of Africa, the greater part of what we now know as Western Astrology became flesh and bone. In the centuries to follow, other elements supplemented and enriched the theory without in any way changing the primary characteristics of Hellenistic astrological theory.

Nevertheless, the belief still prevails among Astrologers today that Astrology based on natal horoscopes was born in Mesopotamia.

Know Thyself, painting by the artist Avgeris Kanatas depicting the spread of Greek ideas around the world[1].

In our historical overview, we will outline the course of Western (Tropical) Astrology to the present day.

First of all, we must distinguish between Astrology based on horoscopes and the informal astrological predictions made by many ancient peoples. The Incas, the Babylonians, the Greeks, the Celtic people of the British Isles, the Native North American Indians and others all examined the dome of the sky above and made some kind of predictions about the future. Usually, the priests or shamans of these peoples read the omens of the

1 Copyright: Vasilis & Maria Avg. Kanata

Gods and portents of things to come in the stars. This is known as omen-based Astrology.

According to Van der Waerden[2], the Astrology of Mesopotamia has 3 phases:

a. The age of omens (up to 630 B.C.)

b. The age of the 12 points of the zodiac in which the passage of Jupiter was predominantly important. Jupiter passes through 1 point of the zodiac each year because it takes 12 years to complete a full circle on the ecliptic (630– 450 B.C.)

c. The age of Astrology based on horoscopes (450 B.C. to the present).

The main arguments supporting the Mesopotamian origin of horoscopic Astrology are:

1. The omens of the 2nd millennium B.C. The best-known omen-based prophecy was found written on a clay tablet, and it predicted that: "if a child is born in the 12th month, he will live long and have many children".
2. The Assyrian tablets with details of eclipses of the sun and the positions of the planets.
3. The predictions of eclipses that were made from the time of the Chaldeans (a Mesopotamian people). From 2000 B.C., Chaldean Astronomers had noticed a relationship between the phases of the Moon and eclipses, and had observed that the eclipses of the Sun and the Moon were repeated close to the same position at a periodic interval of 18 years and 11 + 1/3 days. This periodic cycle is known as the Saros, or the Saros cycle.
4. The first known horoscope in cuneiform script, which dates back to 410 B.C., and the last known of 69 B.C. (according to Enn Kasak, the horoscope predicts the future and character of a child based on the position of the planets).

2 Van Der Waerden, "History of the Zodiac"

5. The horoscope of 410 B.C., which describes the night sky on 29th April of that year, says that: "Nisannu, night of the 14th ... son of Šumu-usur, Šumu-iddina, descendant [...], was born. At that time the Moon was below the pincers of Scorpio, Jupiter in Pisces, Venus in Taurus, Saturn in Cancer, Mars in Gemini. Mercury had set and was not visible. (Things) will be propitious for you." (Rochberg 1998:56)

Based on the above, we can conclude that the people of Mesopotamia did indeed possess a well developed knowledge of Astronomy and Astrology. However, they made predictions which were more in line with omen-based Astrology. They did not have a systematized horoscopic system. It is therefore clear that the respected mathematician Van der Waerden made an assumption which was not supported by the evidence. This assumption received wide acceptance from the astrological community but contributed nothing to the scientific foundation on which his position was based.

If horoscopic Astrology had existed in Mesopotamia then it is certain that Eudoxus of Cnidus (408 – 355 B.C.) would have referred to it in his work Phaenomena. He traveled to Egypt and spent a considerable amount of time there studying celestial phenomena with Egyptian priests. In 525 B.C., Egypt was occupied by the Persians, which brought the two schools of Astronomy in contact with each other.

Aratus of Soli (305 – 240 B.C.), in his poems Phaenomena and Diosemeia (Forecasts), further developed the knowledge of Eudoxus regarding the constellations and the Zodiac. He lived in Soli, Cilicia, and not even he gives us to understand through his work that the peoples of Mesopotamia practiced horoscopic

Astrology. In the poems of Aratus, the 48 ancient Zodiac constellations, as well as many celestial bodies, are precisely described for the first time. In a section of the poem entitled Diosemeia, he makes predictions of an astrological nature which are not based on horoscopic Astrology:

> .....
> look at the edges of the Moon
> ....
> if she is slender and clear about the third day
> she heralds clear skies
> if slender and ruddy we will have winds
> ...
>
> (Excerpt from Diosemeia, by Aratus of Soli)

Hipparchus (190 – 120 B.C.) is considered to be the founding father of Astronomy because he discovered the precessional movement and nutation of the earth around its axis. In other words, he discovered the precession of the equinoxes. He even accurately calculated the movement of point "γ" at the intersection of the celestial equator on the ecliptic, at 26,000 years.

From the time of Hipparchus, more than 200 years passed before the appearance of the Hellenistic Astronomers-Astrologers, the most important of which are Claudius Ptolemy, Vettius Valens and Dorotheus of Sidon, and the discovery of the horoscopic system we now know, which is applied by Western Astrology today.

In particular, Claudius Ptolemy (87 – 165 A.D.) broadly outlined the principles of horoscopic Astrology. In the Almagest (or "The Great Mathematical Treatise"), he explains the theory of the epicycle for the movement of the planets, and in the Tetrabiblos (the Quadripartitum or "Four Books") he explains his astrological theory. An extremely important role in the theoretical training of Claudius Ptolemy was played by the time he spent in the Library of Alexandria, where he had access to most of the known writings of the ancient world.

Claudius Ptolemy already had the scientific achievements and theories of past philosophers and scientists to hand when he was formulating his theory of Astrology. Accordingly, he used:

1. Aristotle's theory of the origin of the Earth from the four elements: fire, water, air, earth
2. Aristotle's theory of the origin of the stars and the planets in the "aether" (the substance of the upper air above the earth)
3. The chart of the Constellations
4. The 12 Constellations of the Zodiac
5. Hipparchus' chart showing approximately 1000 stars
6. Hipparchus' theory of the precession of the Equinoxes
7. The "Astronomica" of Marcus Manilius (an Ionian Greek with a Latin name).
8. The work of Poseidonius (a Greek philosopher and astronomer, 135 – 50 B.C.).

After Ptolemy, other scholars concerned themselves with Astrology included Claudius Galenus (128 – 200 A.D.), and Firmicius Maternus (at the beginning of the 4th century A.D.). The Arab scholars Al-Kindi and Abu Masar (8th century A.D.) came into contact with the Hellenistic legacy after the occupation of Egypt, and further developed it.

They enriched the theory of the "Lots of Fate" of the Greeks (of which there were seven: the Lots - or Parts - of Necessity, Eros, the Demon, Courage, Nemesis, Victory, and Fortune) and expanded them to 97, and later to 143. Many of their elements, in particular the lot of fortune, are still used today.

The great Arab astrologer Al-Biruni drew up precise charts and divided Astrology into 5 domains:

1. Meteorology
2. Plants
3. Animals and people
4. Life and prosperity of the individual
5. Actions and occupations of the individual.

During the Middle Ages, the study and practice of Astrology in Europe was difficult, due to the negative stance taken by the Church. For this reason, its further development passed into the hands of Arab scholars.

Any European involvement in the subject was restricted to the translation of the works of the best-known Arab Astrologers. Between 1120 and 1130 A.D., Adelard of Bath translated the charts of Al-Hovarizmi, and in 1140 Herman of Carinthia translated the Great Introduction to the Science of Astrology by Abu Masar. Claudius Ptolemy's Tetrabiblos was also translated, in 1138 by Plato of Tivoli, whilst in Spain Gerard of Cremona translated Ptolemy's Almagest (the "Great Mathematical Treatise") from the Arabic.

During the Renaissance, the number of people supporting Astrology grew. The voices of the Catholic Church were tempered and new works made their appearance. Central figures of the age include: Marcilio Fitsino (1463-1494), the physician and mathematician Girolamo Cardano (1501-1576), Tomasso Campanella (1568-1639), the humanist theologian Erasmus (1469-1536), the physician Paracelsus (1493-1541), the mathematician John Dee (1527-1608), and the physician and alchemist Nostradamus (1503-1566).

But the best-known Astronomers-Astrologers of the Renaissance were:

1. William Lilly (1602-1681), who worked intensively on "Horary Astrology". Before him, the Italian scholar Guido Bonati had studied this in the 13th century.

   Lilly designed his horoscopes based on the exact time at which he was posed a question by his client. He would base his answers on the horoscope he had constructed, and often his predictions proved to be right. Clients tended to ask simple questions, such as whether a sick wife would survive the next fortnight, or whether a son would return from war.

   Today, Horary Astrology is used occasionally. There are indeed some Astrologers who specialize in these methods.
2. Galileo Galilei (1564-1642), who was the first to discover the 4 major satellite moons of Jupiter: Io, Europa, Ganymede and Callisto. He also discovered the rings of Saturn, the phases of Venus which led him to conclude that it revolved around the Sun, and that the Sun is the center of our planetary system. This confirmed the theory of Aristarchus of Samos, which was copied by Copernicus. All of this was accomplished using a telescope which he himself invented in 1608 (though others attribute the invention of the telescope to the Dutchman Hans Lipperschey). Apart from being a mathematician and an astronomer, Galileo was also an astrologer in the court of the Medici in Florence.
3. The Danish scholar Tycho Brahe (1546-1601) is known for the precise star chart he drew up from the observatory of Uranienborg on the island of Hven. He was a great proponent of Astrology and believed that the planets shape our character.
4. Johannes Kepler (1571-1630) was a colleague of Brahe and a mathematician. By observing the orbit of Mars, he devised his first two laws of motion of the planets.

Johannes Kepler (Portrait by an unknown artist)

I. The planets move in elliptical orbits around the Sun, which is located at one of the foci of the Ellipse.

II. A line joining the Sun and a planet sweeps out over equal intervals of time covering equal areas.

These laws, which apply in nature, were revealed in his book Astronomia Nova. In his work Harmonices Mundi (1619), he developed his third law governing the motion of the planets:

III. The square of the orbital period of the planets is directly proportional to the cube of the semi-major axes of their orbits.

Kepler was closely involved in Astrology and was able to earn a living from it.

5. Isaac Newton (1643-1727) revealed the law of universal gravitation in his *Mathematical Principles of Natural Philosophy* (1687). It is here that the notion of the circumambulation of the planets around the Sun acquires a meaning. Together with the three laws of Kepler, Astronomy finally became established as a science.
   Despite this, Newton was also an alchemist and an astrologer, which was surprising to his contemporaries, scientists such as Edmond Halley.
   With their discoveries, Newton and Kepler exposed mysticism and refuted the theory of the motion of the planets proposed by Claudius Ptolemy. Thus, they threw Astrology into oblivion for more than two centuries.

From that time until the present day, very little has been added to astrological theory which is truly worth mentioning.
In this book, those who are familiar with Western Astrology can go straight to the second part, which describes the Astrological Theory of the 13 Signs of the Zodiac. The first part principally describes uranographic coordinate systems, and subsequently the methodology of Western Astrologers, critiquing and analyzing the nature of the problem created by their theoretical foundations.

PART 1

WESTERN ASTROLOGY

Chapter 1

Fundamentals of Uranography and Astrology

In order to gain further insight into the concepts of Astrology, first of all we must have an understanding of the position and shape of the celestial sphere and the coordinates we employ to measure the positions of celestial bodies.

The key factor to be taken into account is the shape of the sky above us. We regard it as being spherical, irrespective of the distance between any of the celestial bodies: planets, satellites and galaxies. We therefore assume that our Earth (being nearly spherical) is contained within another sphere and that all stellar objects are located on the latter (see Figure 1-1 on the following page). If the plane defined by the Earth's Equator is extended outwards, it will intersect the celestial sphere and define another circle: the Celestial Equator. If we imagine the rotational axis of the Earth to extend outwards into space then the point at which this extension will penetrate the celestial sphere is at the tail end of Ursa Minor, beside the star known as the pole star (the North Celestial Pole, shown in the figure).

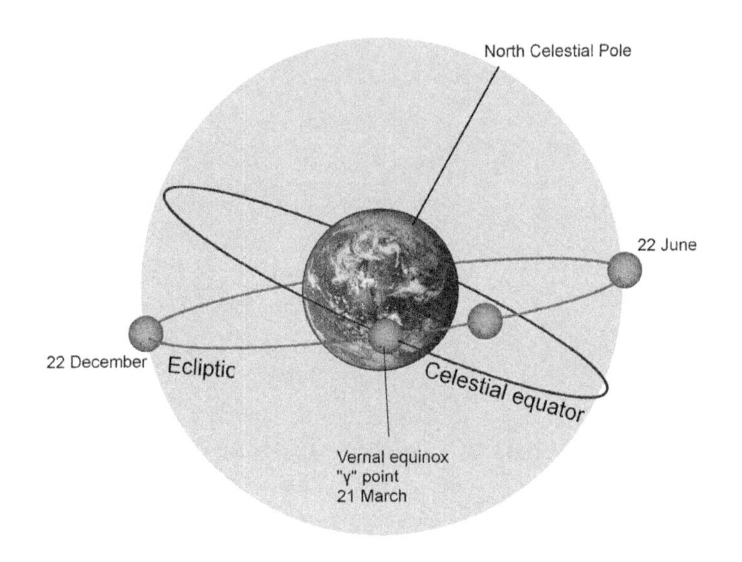

Figure 1-1: Precession of the equinoxes (point 'γ'). This diagram shows the location of point γ (Vernal Equinox). The Earth's axis moves in the same way as the axis of a spinning top, in a cycle which spans a precessional period of 25,920 years. Drawing by V. Kanatas based on NASA images of the Earth and the Sun.

Similar to the Earth's latitude and longitude are the Declination and Right Ascension in the celestial sphere. However, there is no fixed point of reference in the sky similar to that of Greenwich on Earth. We therefore employ a point on the Celestial Equator called the 'γ' point.

But before determining point 'γ', we must first consider the Ecliptic, another imaginary circle on the celestial sphere. The ecliptic is the Sun's apparent annual path across the sky. The Earth rotates around the Sun in 365 days, and its axis is inclined in relation to the Earth's orbital plane at a precise angle of exactly 23.5°. In the above figure, imagine that the Earth remains at its current tilt whilst maintaining a horizontal orbit around the Sun. It therefore travels to complete a full circle in 365 days and its axis always points to the same point in the sky (the pole star).

When we observe the sky from Earth, the Sun seems to orbit on the Ecliptic and indeed to move from West to East, at an approximate speed of one degree (1°) each day, since it completes a journey of 360° within 365 days.

The points at which the Celestial Equator intersects the Ecliptic are γ and γ'. Points γ and γ' are situated in the Constellations of Pisces and Virgo respectively. Celestial longitude is measured between γ and the East (in degrees) whilst celestial latitude is measured from the celestial Equator to the North or South Celestial Pole.

If we consider the ecliptic to be the fundamental reference circle, then we shift to the Ecliptic Coordinate System. The zero point in this system is also point γ, although ecliptic longitude is measured from point γ to the east on the ecliptic, whilst the ecliptic latitude is measured from the ecliptic to the North or South Ecliptic Pole.

All of the above seems fairly reasonable, but there is a fundamental problem. There is an annual shift in point γ of 50.2" (seconds of a degree) per year. This is equivalent to approximately one degree each 72 years, with a full circle being completed within about 25,920 years.

This occurs because the shape of the Earth is that of an oblate spheroid, and thus differential gravitational forces are generated close to the Equator. These forces are due to the combined impact of the Sun, the Moon and the planets. Hence, the Earth orbits as a spinning top, making a slight precessional motion accompanied by nutation (wobbling) in relation to its axis. This effect is known as the "Precession of the Equinoxes" or the precession of point γ.

If the Earth were a single point, then we could see the surrounding sky at its full length and width, and we could observe the celestial equator; the ecliptic and the Poles. As we always remain on the Earth's surface, half of the sky is hidden by the horizon. Depending on latitude, time and season, the appearance of the sky will change as shown in the following figures:

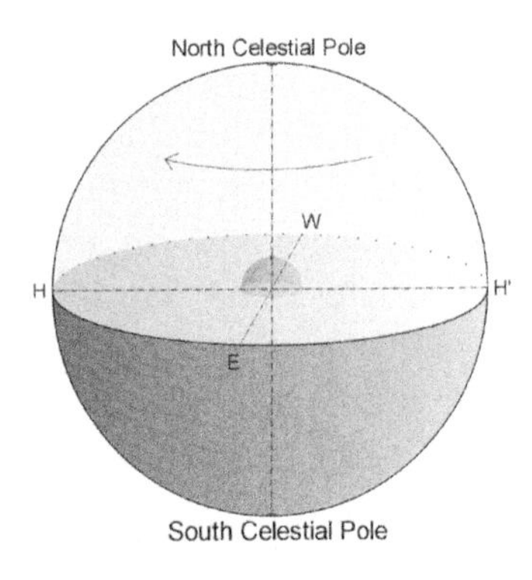

Figure 1-2:
Observer at the North Pole (Figure by User CAV[3])

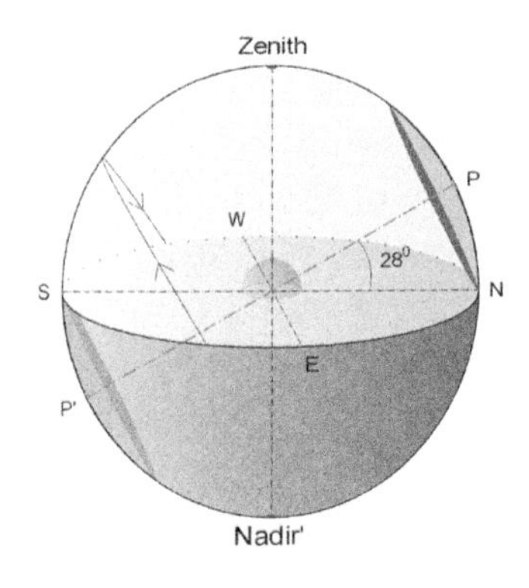

Figure 1-3:
Observer at latitude 28° North (Figure by User CAV[4])

I. The figure 1-2 shows the sky as seen by an observer situated at the North Pole. The beige plane corresponds to the observer's horizon. The Pole Star is located at the Zenith;

3 User CAV, owner of the intellectual property rights to this work, releases such work to the public domain. Such release is applicable worldwide.
4 Ibid.

all Constellations of the Celestial Sphere north of the Equator are visible and rotate in the direction of the arrow, although they never rise or set!

II. Figure 1-3 shows the dome of the sky as seen by an observer situated at 28° latitude north of the Equator. All Constellations located at angular distances from 62° degrees (90°-28° = 62°) to 90° north of the celestial equator are circumpolar; meaning that they are always visible throughout the night at latitude 28° north. This region is depicted near point P in the figure. Similarly, all Celestial Constellations with Latitudes between -62° and -90° South are invisible (below the horizon) and are shown near point P' in the figure. The other Constellations are non-circumpolar, i.e. they may or may not be visible depending on time and season.

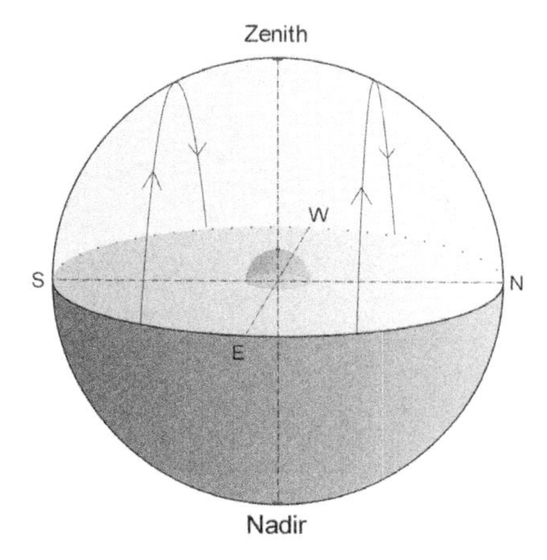

Figure 1-4: Observer at the Equator (Figure by User CAV[5])

III. Lastly, for an observer situated at the Earth's Equator, the South – North axis (SN, figure 1-4) is located on the plane of the horizon (shown in beige) and all Constellations rise and set

5 Ibid.

depending on season and time.
The 13 constellations of the Zodiac occupy positions directly over the ecliptic. The Earth actually moves through these Constellations on its annual orbit as seen from the Sun, although by convention we say exactly the opposite (i.e. that the Sun crosses their path as it orbits around the Earth). It should be borne in mind that the daily rotation of the Earth is not connected to its annual motion.

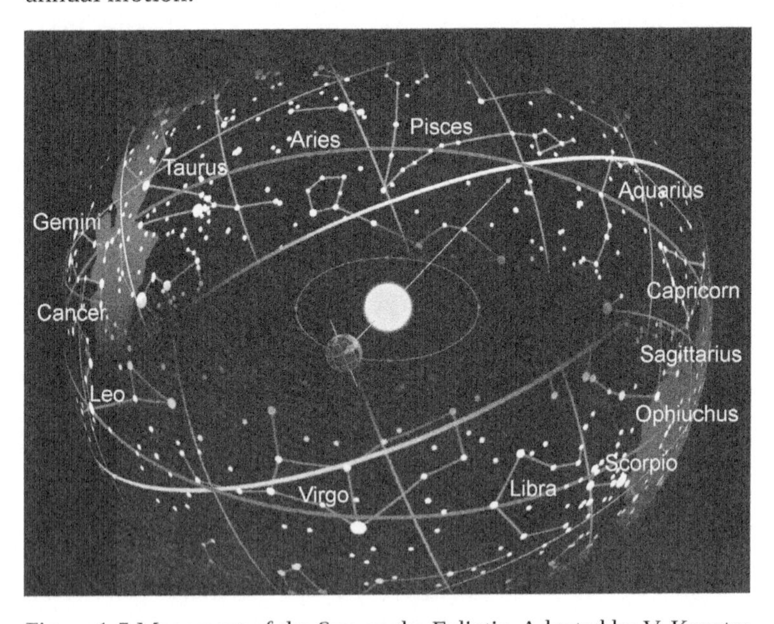

Figure 1-5 Movement of the Sun on the Ecliptic. Adapted by V. Kanatas to show names of constellations, from an original design by Tau'olunga[6]

6 License to copy, distribute and/or modify this image is granted under the terms of the GNU Free Documentation License (GFDL), Version 1.2 or any newer version published by the Free Software Foundation, without Unchanged Sections, and without Front or Back Cover texts. A copy of the license is contained on the webpage under the title GNU Free Documentation License

http://www.gnu.org/copyleft/fdl.html GFDL GNU Free Documentation The

Now carefully observe the 13 Constellations of the Zodiac as the Sun moves along the Ecliptic (the grey line throught the Zodiac Constellations in the diagram). Exactly behind the Sun as we observe it from Earth is the Zodiac representing the region where the Sun is located on the given day. The Sun remains in each Zodiac Constellation from 6.5 to 44 days. Modern science is easily capable of precisely determining the position of the Sun within the boundaries of the Zodiac Constellations.

Chapter 2

The Nature of the Problem

The Astrology of the 13 Signs of the Zodiac conflicts as much with "Western" (Tropical) Astrology as it does with "Indian" (Sidereal) Astrology.

What was proposed by the ancient Greeks and was perfected as a theory by Claudius Ptolemy in the 2nd century B.C., we call Western Astrology.

At that time, Astronomy and Astrology were of parallel importance and were closely connected. Astronomy as a science was mainly concerned with the position of the constellations in the sky, the distances of the Moon and the planets from our Earth, the eclipses of the Sun and the Moon, and the interpretation of the movement of the planets in the sky. Astrology, in its turn, made predictions about the weather, crops, people's lives and the outcome of wars. That is, it was characterized by forecasts of the future. Almost all Astronomers were also Astrologers. Thus, on the one hand, Claudius Ptolemy developed his theory known as the "theory of epicycles" to interpret the movement of the planets, and on the other, from an astrological perspective, he developed a method of formulating predictions about the life and future of each of us.

The astrological theory of Ptolemy is based on a Horoscope, a circular chart with 12 equal arcs. The circle on the chart symbolizes the ecliptic; that is, the annual orbit of the Sun around the dome of the sky. Thus, a horoscope mainly composed of the position of the Sun, the planets and the Moon at the moment of their birth can be constructed for any person.

The Chart, as based on Ptolemy's theory, contains only the 12 Zodiac constellations and the positions of the planets. The Sun, the Moon and the planets move within a belt which appears in the form of a strip wrapped around a large sphere. In the center of this belt is a circle called the ecliptic which indicates the orbit of the Sun around the dome of the sky as it appears from the Earth (See figure 1-5 in the previous chapter).

Ptolemy divided this belt into 12 equal sections of 30°, with the 12 Zodiac constellations equally distributed around it. As we shall see below, there are many problems to be resolved here.

For a person born on 5 October, notice the symbol for the Sun in figure 2-1: ⊙, the following observations can be made:

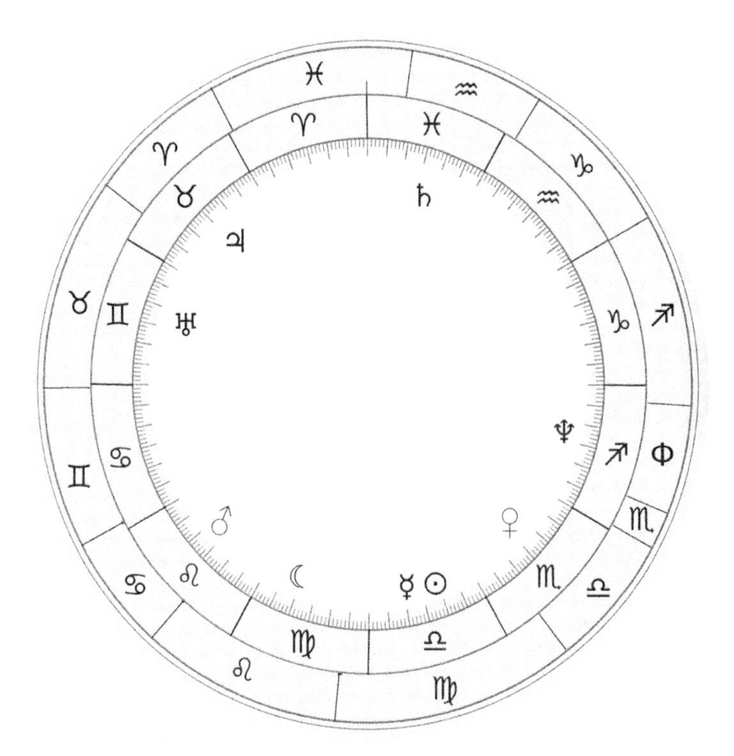

Figure 2-1: The ring of Western Astrology (the inner ring), and the ring representing the actual distribution of the 13 constellations of the Zodiac (outer ring). Φ symbolizes Ophiuchus. Design by V. Kanatas

In Western Astrology his Zodiac Sign is Libra, (inner circle of figure 2-1), in Indian Astrology he's Virgo and in the Astrology of the 13 Zodiac signs, also Virgo (outer circle). His Ascendant would be Capricorn in Western Astrology and Sagittarius in Indian Astrology. We shall see below why it is best to calculate the Ascendant from the position of the Moon ☾. On the basis of this, the Ascendant would be Leo in the Astrology of the 13 Signs of the Zodiac.

The 5 planets that Claudius Ptolemy used to consider for his predictions are in the following positions:

	Western Astrology	Astrology of the 13 Signs of the Zodiac
Mercury ☿:	Libra ♎	Virgo ♍
Venus ♀:	Scorpio ♏	Libra ♎
Mars ♂:	Leo ♌	Cancer ♋
Jupiter ♃:	Taurus ♉	Aries ♈
Saturn ♄:	Pisces ♓	Aquarius ♒

All well and good, you may say, it's just a different approach. No! It is not a question of approach. It is a question of fact and objectivity. Only in 13 Zodiac Astrology do the positions of the planets coincide with their actual positions. Western Astrology is unable to offer an explanation for this.

Not even Indian Astrology can claim to be close to the truth because, on the one hand, it theorizes that the Zodiac constellations occupy a 30° arc on the ecliptic – which is incorrect – and on the other it rejects the constellation of Ophiuchus which, occupying an arc length of 18.5° (degrees) on the ecliptic, must be taken into account in every prediction.

The Zodiac circle in Indian or Vedic Astrology follows the movement of point γ in the sky. It theorizes that the Zodiac cycle of Tropical (Western) Astrology was identical to the Indian Astrology of 285 A.D. Since that time, however, the Zodiac cycle of Western Astrology has remained 50.2" of a degree behind. Thus, 1,726 years have passed from 285 A.D. to the present (the year 2011), and therefore point γ has moved 1726 X 50.2" = 86,645.2", that is, 86,645.2/3600 = 24.07° approximately. These 24.07° represent the difference between Western and Indian Astrology. The cycle of Indian Astrology in relation to the actual cycle of the 13 Constellations of the Zodiac, which reflects the true circumstances, is shown below:

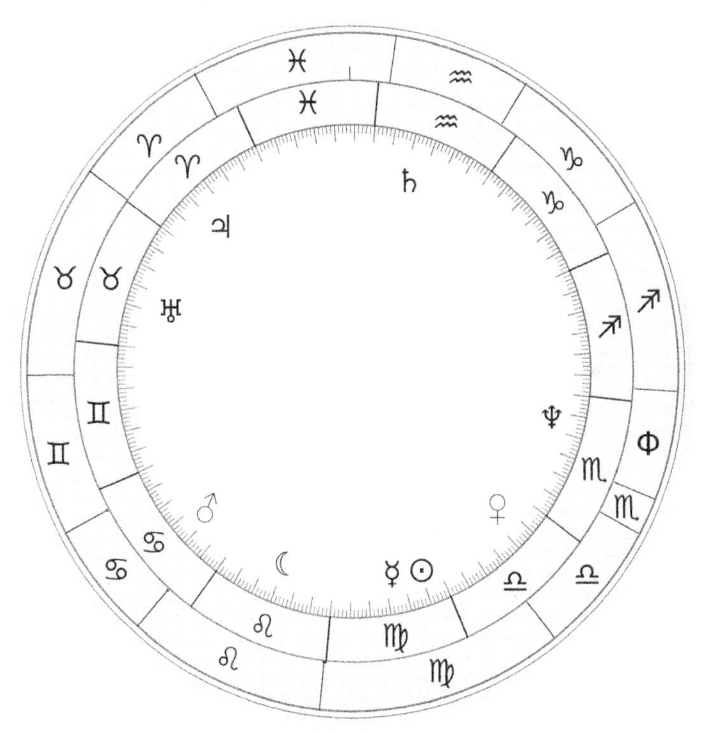

Figure 2-2: The ring of Indian or Vedic Astrology (the inner ring), and the ring representing the actual distribution of the 13 constellations of the Zodiac (outer ring). Φ symbolizes Ophiuchus. Design by V. Kanatas

In summary:

1. All the premises of traditional Western (Tropical) Astrology are misplaced.
2. Most elements of Eastern or Stellar (Sidereal) Astrology are erroneous. That is, it divides the Zodiac into equal parts along the ecliptic which is incorrect (even if this is modified to take into account the precession of the equinoxes). It does not take Ophiuchus into account (a second mistake). It also theorizes that the planets govern the constellations of the Zodiac (a third mistake).
3. Everything falls into place with 13 Zodiac Astrology, as we shall establish in detail in the second part of this book.

Let us consider an example before we proceed to examine the configurations which demonstrate the delusions of Western Astrology.

Imagine a person loves the sea and wants to swim in the same places as the ancients did. The coastline, however, has moved position by 3 km in comparison with the coastline in antiquity. Because our swimmer knows the exact point on the ancient coastline, he proceeds to go there, pretending to swim in what is now dry land and fields.

This is precisely what today's Western Astrologers do. They "pretend" that your Zodiac sign is Scorpio although it is Libra; they "pretend" that the planet Jupiter is in Aries although it is in Pisces.

The main problem for so-called Western Astrology is the precession of the equinoxes. The sky above has changed, but the Astrologers still "see" it as their ancestors did, more than 2,094 years ago!

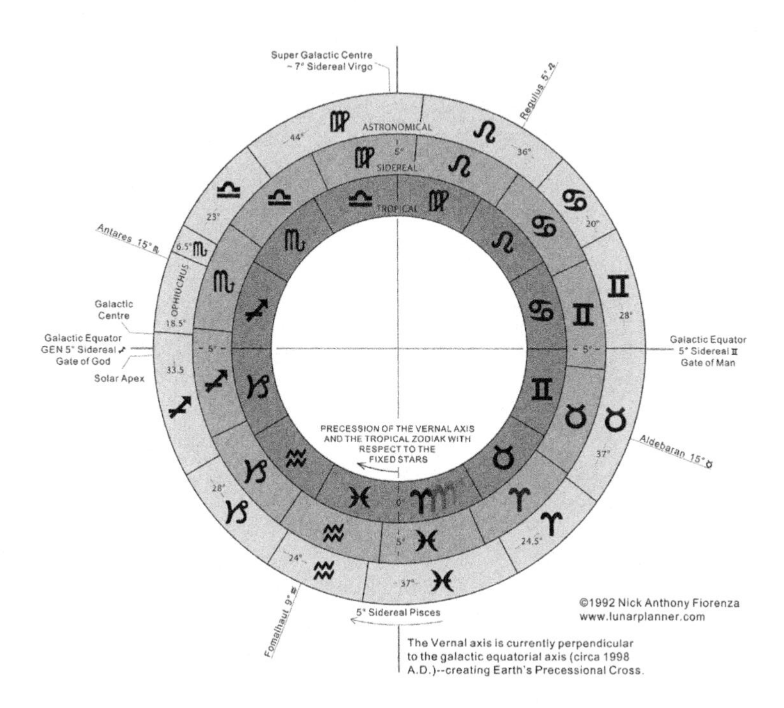

Figure 2-3: The three Zodiac Circles. The inner ring is that of Western Astrology, the middle ring is that of Indian Astrology, and the outer ring represents the true Zodiac Circle (used by 13 Zodiac Astrology). In contrast with the two previous diagrams, point γ is located at the bottom of the schema. Work by Nick Anthony. Copyright © Nick Anthony 1992. Published with the permission of the creator.

Chapter 3

How Western Astrologers Work.

1. **Assumptions**

Western Astrology borrows and copies most of its assumptions from Ancient Greek Astrology. This condensation of astrological theory is contained in the Tetrabiblos of Claudius Ptolemy, the Greek astronomer and astrologer from Alexandria in Egypt (87-165 B.C.).

Presented here are the twenty assumptions on which the predictions of Western Astrology are based. The three first assumptions also comprise the Aristotelian theory of the Earth and our cosmos.

1st Assumption: The four elements from which the world (our Earth) is made are fire, water, earth and air.

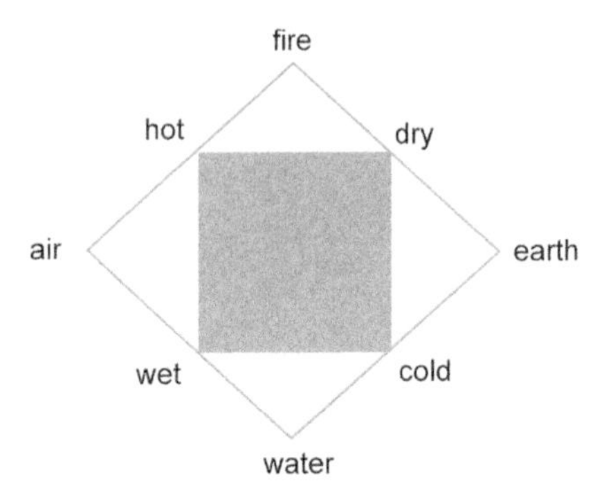

Figure 3-1: Elements and qualities

2nd Assumption: The four qualities arising from the above elements are: hot, cold, dry and wet.

3rd Assumption: The celestial heavens are made of a fifth element, aether. The ethereal spheres above the Earth are: the Sun, the Moon, Mercury, Venus, Mars, Jupiter, Saturn and the fixed stars. Each of the ethereal spheres has its own rotation.

4th Assumption: The Sun and the Moon have a significant impact on the Earth and its people. The remaining planets also exert their influence in specific ways. The Sun heats and dries. The Moon creates moisture, Saturn cools and dries, Mars dries and burns. Jupiter is a temperate creative force, providing warmth and moisture accordingly. Venus is similar to Jupiter, and Mercury is alternately a drying force or a bringer of moisture.

5th Assumption: The planets (together with the Sun, which was considered to be a planet) are categorized as male or female.

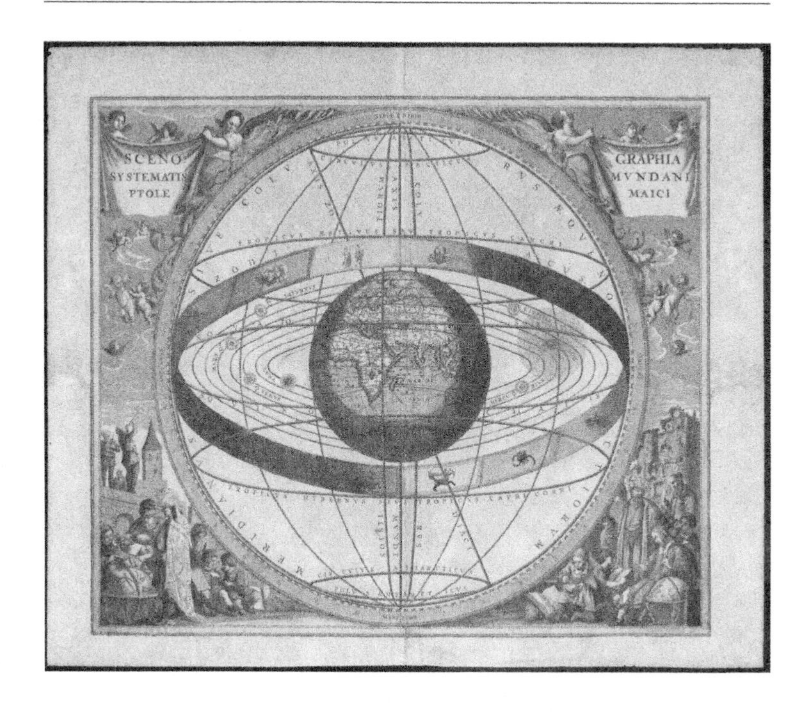

Figure 3-2: The orbits of the planets according to the Ptolemaic Systems, with the Earth at the center. Picture entitled Scenographia Systematis Mundani Ptolemaici by Johannes van Loon (1611-1686)

6th Assumption: The planets are divided into two categories: the favorable and the unfavorable.

7th Assumption: The planets are characterized as either diurnal or nocturnal.

8th Assumption: The effect of the planets changes according to the aspects (angles) they form between each other and the Sun.

9th Assumption: The fixed stars have a specific effect directly comparable to that of the influence of the planets (e.g. The star Spica - α or Alpha Virginis - the brightest star in Virgo, has the same effect as Venus and the moderated effect of Mars).

10th Assumption: Both the seasons of the year and the angles of the horizon affect the prediction.

11th Assumption: The signs of the Zodiac are categorized as Tropical, Equinoctial, Fixed and Bicorporeal. Tropical: Cancer and Capricorn. Equinoctial: Aries and Libra. Fixed: Taurus, Leo, Scorpio and Aquarius. Bicorporeal: Gemini, Virgo, Sagittarius, Pisces.
Under the 11th assumption, the Tropical and Equinoctial signs are sometimes merged into one category by Western Astrologers. This gives a new category of "Cardinal" (impulsive) signs: Cancer, Capricorn, Aries, and Libra (the fixed and bicorporeal categories remain the same).

12th Assumption: The Signs of the Zodiac are categorized as male or female:
Male: Aries, Gemini, Leo, Libra, Sagittarius, Aquarius
Female: Taurus, Cancer, Virgo, Scorpio, Capricorn, Pisces

13th Assumption: Each planet has at least one sign of the Zodiac as its own planetary house, where it is considered to reside "permanently". The houses of the planets are the following:

Sun: Leo
Moon: Cancer
Saturn: Capricorn, Aquarius
Jupiter: Sagittarius, Pisces
Mars: Aries, Scorpio
Venus: Libra, Taurus
Mercury: Gemini, Virgo

14th Assumption: The Signs of the Zodiac are divided into submissive and dominant. The summer (aestival) semi-cycle incorporates the dominant and the winter (hyemal) semi-cycle the submissive.

15th Assumption: The Signs of the Zodiac are divided into equivalent or otherwise. Equivalent signs are those directly facing each other. They are known as equivalent because when one rises the other sets.

16th Assumption: All zodiac constellations which do not have a relationship between each other of the above type are disjointed.

17th Assumption: The Signs of the Zodiac have familial relationships between each other based on their specific positions:

First of all, those which are at a distance of 180° (degrees) (opposite) from each other are related; that is, for each pair of Zodiac constellations, there are 6 complementary relationships:

Aries-Libra
Taurus-Scorpio
Gemini-Sagittarius
Cancer-Capricorn
Leo-Aquarius
Virgo-Pisces

Secondly, those which are separated by 120° (degrees) – in a triangular position or Trine - are said to be in harmonious aspect.
There are 4 Triplicities:
Aries-Leo-Sagittarius (rulers: the Sun by day and Jupiter by night)
Taurus-Virgo-Capricorn (rulers: Venus by day and the Moon by night)
Gemini-Libra-Aquarius (rulers: Saturn by day and Mercury by night)
Cancer-Scorpio-Pisces (rulers: Mars together with Venus by day and the Moon at night)

Thirdly, those forming a quartile are said to be in non-harmonious (tense) aspects, and fourthly, those forming a sextile, or hexagon, like the trine, are said to be in harmonious aspect.

18th Assumption: The constellation which is in ascendance in a specific location at the moment of a person's birth is known as the Ascendant, and is of great consequence for his/her character. On the basis of the Ascendant, the Houses of the Natal Horoscope are determined.
The above assumptions derive directly from Claudius Ptolemy's Tetrabiblos, with the exception of the first three, which, though accepted by Ptolemy, are the convictions of Aristotle.
Astrologers of the Middle Ages further developed the system of Ascendant Houses. An explanation of the way in which the system of Houses works is presented below.

19th Assumption: Starting from the horoscopic ascendant the 12 houses, considered to represent the various areas of human existence, are constructed. The houses represent the following:

Each house represents an area of earthly human activity, such as finances, love life, etc.

1st House: The East (rising), the ego, the beginning. Physical appearance and traits, health, constitution.

2nd House: Security, belongings, personal property. Physical or emotional possessiveness.

3rd House: Communication, understanding. Environment, surroundings, neighborhood, family. Journeys, excursions, travel. Studies, lessons, education, training.

4th House: The South. Personal foundations and roots. Ancestry, parents, mother, family, the home. Real estate property, land, fields, homeland.

5th House: Holidays, vacations, unemployment, days off, breaks. Fun, pleasure, celebrations, feasts. Relaxation, rest. Romance, flirtation. Games, children, childhood.

6th House: Matters of health and illness. Work-related matters, profession, jobs, effort, occupation.

7th House: The West (setting). Others, opposites. The other half. The life partner, confidante. Open confrontation, conflict, disagreement.

8th House: Transformations, death, change. Sexual activity. Financial benefits and partnerships.

9th House: Research, exploration. Higher education and universities. Religion, philosophy and intellectual pursuits. Wandering, foreign travel and long journeys. Expansion of horizons (physical and intellectual).

10th House: The North. The path of life, career. Advancement, social climbing, acquiring reputation. Administration and government. Persons of high standing.

11th House: Groups and associations. Companies, federations. Friendship, companions, sociability. Ambitions and desires.

12th House: Isolation, introversion. The subconscious. Hidden things, secrets. Despair, troubles, suffering.

Astrologers have, since the 18th Century, added the more recently discovered planets: Uranus (discovered in 1781), Neptune (1846), Pluto (1930) and Chiron, which was discovered in 1977.

20th Assumption: The newly-discovered planets affect our horoscope in combination with those already known.

2. Construction of the Western Horoscope

We can now take an analytical look at the way in which the Astrologers of Western Astrology proceed to construct a person's natal horoscope.

Dimitris was born in Athens on 29/03/1980 at 1.00 p.m. We intend to use his birth data to construct a Western Astrology Horoscope.

I. We first use a pair of compasses to draw a circle, which we then divide into twelve equal parts, and then, for greater accuracy, divide the whole into 360 subdivisions (degrees).

Having drawn the circle with its subdivisions we then need to make an extensive search of the astrological tables of traditional Astrology, in order to determine the stellar year, the positions of the planets, the ascendant, the culmination (Midheaven – M.C.). The entire exercise is a perfect example of going to a great deal of trouble for nothing, since, as we shall prove, it is all based on completely false premises.

However, the subsequent procedure adopted is as follows:

a. We would record, for example, the latitude and longitude of Dimitris' place of birth, in this case Athens, which is at eastern latitude 23°45'E and northern longitude 37°54'N.

b. Next, we would convert his time of birth (29/3/1980, at 13.00 h) to Greenwich Mean Time (GMT), taking summer (daylight saving) time into account. GMT is 11.00 a.m. In 1980 summer time began on Sunday 6th April, so taking this into account does not change the time of birth.

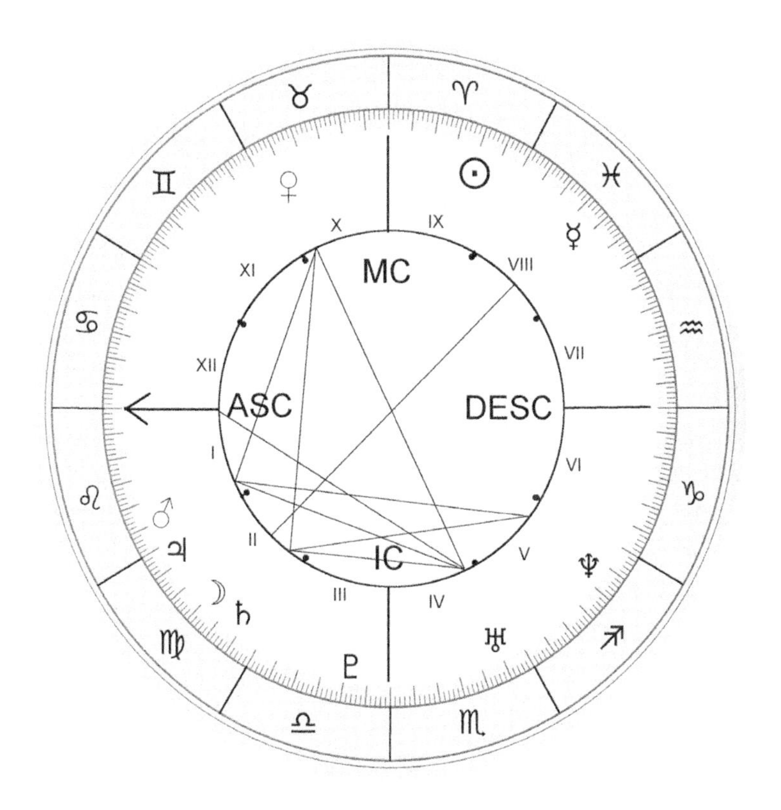

Figure 3-3: Construction of Dimitri's Natal Horoscope (born in Athens, on 29/3/1980 at 13.00), based on the principles of Western Astrology (equal house system).

c. The Horoscope is determined by converting the time of birth to Stellar Time (ST). This conversion is based on the charts of each year:
The GMT to Stellar Time conversion tables for 29/3/1980 give us: (where h = hours, m = minutes and s = seconds)

12h 24m 21s

To this is added a correction of 1m 51s, giving us:

12h 26m 11s

This is the Stellar Time for 29/3/1980 at 00:00 GMT. For the time 11:00am we add 11 hours to the Stellar Time above to give us:

23h 26m 11s

To this we add a correction of 2 minutes because Stellar Time is 4 minutes ahead per 24 hour period, that is, for 11 hours, approximately 2 minutes.

The Stellar Time becomes:

23h 28m 11s

This is the stellar time equivalent to GMT which must be converted to the stellar time for Athens. This is done as follows:

Athens is at Eastern latitude 23°45'E. For this value the correction is + 1h 35m.

Stellar time Athens with this addition becomes:

25h 3m 11s

We subtract 24 hours to give the final value:

1h 3m 11s

d. The Ascendant is calculated by reference to the table of houses for longitudes north of the Equator. Thus, in the ST columns we would look for the time 1h 03m for longitude 37°54'N where we see the Ascendant in Leo at 0.09°.

e. We place the Ascendant to the left-hand side of the circle and the subdivisions so that 0.09 ° in Leo is on the left-hand side, as shown in Figure 3-3.

f. All the signs of the Zodiac are placed around the outer circle starting from the Ascendant sign moving in an anticlockwise direction. Note that this starts from 0.09° degrees in Leo.

g. The positions of the planets around the circle arise from other tables (Astrological Almanacs), which give their positions for each date at 00:00 GMT. Here, new calculations are required to correct the positions of the Sun, the Moon and the planets. After the new calculations have been made, we find that the Sun is located at 8.55° in Aries and the remaining planets as shown in the figure above.

h. Next, the aspects of the planets are calculated (oppositions, conjunctions, trines, quartiles, and sextiles) on the basis of assumptions made.
Aspect assumptions:
conjunction, 8° tolerance
opposition, 8° tolerance
trine, 8° tolerance
quartile, 8° tolerance
sextile, 6° tolerance

The conjunctions, oppositions, trines, quartiles and sextiles are drawn up in accordance with the principles described above.

i. Starting with the Ascendant, we construct a new circle containing 12 sections (equal or unequal according to the system followed by each astrologer) in an anticlockwise direction. These 12 sections constitute the Houses from 1 to 12, and these are usually symbolized by Latin numerals.

3. The Astrological Houses

The division of the ecliptic into 12 arcs, in a manner that makes Astrological prediction more complicated, creates what are called Astrological Houses.

There are many systems for dividing the Houses, but they are all based on the Ascendant. The theory of the Houses was added to Astrology during the Middle Ages.

Different House systems were constructed by Placidus (1688), Regiomontanus and Campanus. The most predominant system is that of Equal Houses.

a. The Equal House System

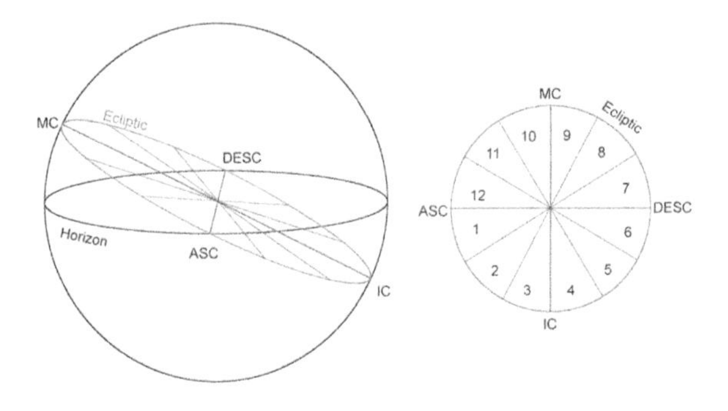

Figure 3-4: The Equal House System. Design by Vasilis Kanatas.

In the left-hand figure above, there are two circles separating the celestial sphere (the large circle containing the other two is to give perspective). The almost horizontal circle is the horizon at the person's time of birth. The circle which is divided into 12 sections is the ecliptic. On the ecliptic is the Ascendant (Asc), the Midheaven (MC – Medium Coeli), the Descendant (Desc), and the Nadir (IC – Imum Coeli).

Having calculated the Ascendant we divide the ecliptic into 30° degree arcs which represent the Houses 1 to 12.

b. The Campanus (1220 – 1296) System

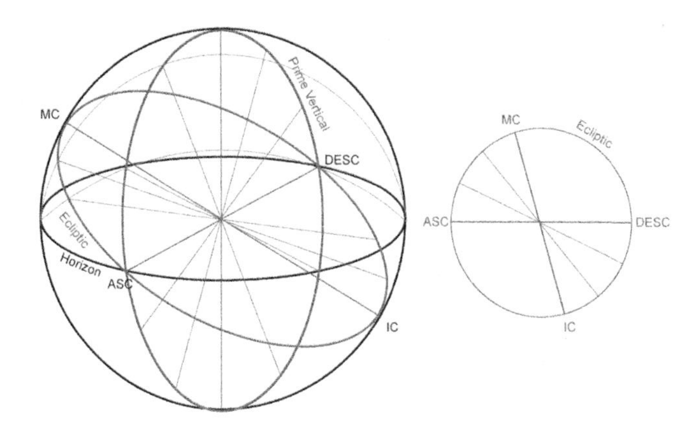

Figure 3-5: The system for division of the Houses by Johannes Campanus. Design by V. Kanatas.

The construction of the Campanus House System is a little more complex. For the time of birth, a circle is drawn vertical to the horizon with the Ascendant in the East. This circle is divided into equal 30° degree sections. Next we construct arcs from North to South such that they pass through the points at which the vertical circle intersects the sphere. As a result of this, the circle on the ecliptic will be divided into unequal sections as shown in figure 3-5 to the right.

c. The Regiomontanus (1436 – 1476) System

The celestial equator is divided into 12 equal sections. These sections are projected onto the ecliptic as follows: A circle from North to South is drawn for each section such that it passes through the points of contact of the celestial equator with the celestial sphere. These circles in their turn divide the ecliptic into 12 unequal sections.

4. How predictions are made in Western Astrology

We have examined the assumptions based upon which Western Astrologers divide the Houses and construct the Horoscope. So how do they make their predictions?

Let's see what the renowned Astrologers Julia and Derek Parker have to say in their book "Astrology":

"Now rely on the key words for each planet, house and signs of the zodiac, and use these to make short sentences. For example, if the Sun is in Cancer in the seventh house: You will express yourself (Sun) very protectively and sensitively (Cancer) towards your companions (7th House)".

Dimitris' Natal Horoscope:
(Born in Athens on 29/3/1980 at 13.00)

"Dimitris' soul realizes its existence in Aries. He is aware of his ego. His behavior is enthusiastic, dynamic and hyperactive. He believes in the existence of justice which will allow him to realize his dreams.

The driving force of his character is affected by springtime. He is among the pioneers of the Zodiac circle. He is in the driver's seat.

His Ascendant in Leo gives him energy and brilliance. He is noble, ambitious and generous. He loves children. He has strong feelings for or against others.

The Moon in Virgo makes him emotionally shy, yet willing to help those around him.

Mercury in Pisces makes him insightful and highly imaginative.

Venus in Taurus is considered to be in her own House and thus is free to express herself without inhibition. Passion is absent from his relationships; something which is replaced by faithfulness and calm".

In closing this chapter on the predictions of Western Astrology, it must be said that we will soon see below that all of this is merely hot air, for the simple reason that the supposed positions of the planets and the constellations of the Zodiac as employed by Western Astrologers do not in any way reflect their true positions.

Chapter 4

The Rejection of Western Astrology

1. Which of the assumptions apply?

Let us examine one by one the assumptions of Western Astrology as presented in the previous chapter:

1st Assumption: *The four elements from which the world (our Earth) is made are fire, water, earth and air.*

Response: This is the first myth to collapse under 13 Zodiac Sign Astrology. It is patently obvious that this is untrue. Science tells us that our world is comprised of molecules constructed from atoms. Atoms are constructed from neutrons, protons and electrons, which in turn are constructed from quarks.

2nd Assumption: *The four qualities arising from the above elements are: hot, cold, dry, and wet.*

Response: As assumption 1 does not apply, neither does 2, since it is based on 1.

3rd Assumption: *The celestial heavens are made of a fifth element, aether. The ethereal spheres above the Earth are: the Sun, the Moon, Mercury, Venus, Mars, Jupiter, Saturn and the fixed stars. Each of the ethereal spheres has its own revolution.*

Response: Today we know from space travel and research that the planets and the stars are made from the same types of particles that make up our Earth. We also know that the Sun is not a planet but a star, containing more than 99% of the mass of our solar system, here too, overturning the notions of Western Astrology.

Based on Kepler's laws, all the planets revolve around the Sun:

1. The planets move in elliptical orbits around the Sun, which is located at one of the 2 foci of the Ellipse.
2. Over the same periods of time the planets cover equivalent distances.
3. The squares of the orbital period of the planets are directly proportional to the cube of the semi-major axes of their orbits.

Therefore assumption 3 **does not apply.**

4th ***Assumption:*** *The Sun and the Moon have a significant impact on the Earth and its people. The remaining planets also exert their influence in specific ways. The Sun heats and dries. The Moon creates moisture, Saturn cools and dries, Mars dries and burns, Jupiter is a temperate creative force, providing warmth and moisture accordingly. Venus is similar to Jupiter and Mercury is alternately a drying force or a bringer of moisture.*

Response: This assumption can be generally applied to the Sun, the Moon and the planets, without necessarily implying acceptance of the details noted by Ptolemy – that they have a drying, warming or temperate creative power. We shall have more to say about this in the chapters referring to the Sun, Moon and planets in the 2nd part of the book.

5th ***Assumption:*** *The planets (together with the Sun, which was considered to be a planet) are categorized as male or female.*

Response: There is no scientific evidence to support the personification of the planets or their division into male and female categories. Therefore assumption 5 is mistaken.

6th ***Assumption:*** *The planets are divided into two categories: the favorable and the unfavorable.*

Response: There is no scientific evidence to support such a suggestion. Therefore this is also mistaken. (see the reason for rejecting Assumption 5).

7th ***Assumption:*** *The planets are characterized as either diurnal or nocturnal.*

Response: There are no diurnal or nocturnal planets. All planets exist and exert influence both day and night.

8th Assumption: *The effect of the planets changes according to the aspects (angles) they form between each other and the Sun.*

Response: This position is partially correct.

9th Assumption: *The fixed stars have a specific effect directly comparable to that of the influence of the planets. (e.g. The star Spica - or Alpha Virginis - the brightest star in Virgo, has the same effect as Venus and the moderated effect of Mars).*

Response: This position is entirely arbitrary and without scientific foundation.

10th Assumption: *Both the seasons of the year and the angles of the horizon affect the prediction.*

Response: This assumption cannot be characterized as incorrect; we will examine it within the framework of our theory in Chapter 1 of Part 2.

11th Assumption: The signs of the Zodiac are categorized as Tropical, Equinoctial, Fixed and Bicorporeal.
Tropical: Cancer and Capricorn. Equinoctial: Aries and Libra. Fixed: Taurus, Leo, Scorpio and Aquarius. Bicorporeal: Gemini, Virgo, Sagittarius, Pisces.
Under the 11th assumption, the Tropical and Equinoctial signs are sometimes merged into one category by Western Astrologers. This gives a new category of "Cardinal" (impulsive) signs: Cancer, Capricorn, Aries, and Libra (the fixed and bicorporeal categories remain the same).

Response: Due to the precession of the equinoxes the positions of the zodiac constellations on the ecliptic have been displaced and the above system of categorization does not apply. Today the Tropical Zodiac constellations are: Pisces and Virgo. Equinoctial: Taurus and Sagittarius (Therefore the 'Cardinal' - impulsive - signs are: Pisces, Virgo, Taurus and Sagittarius). Fixed: Aries, Gemini, Libra and Capricorn. Bicorporeal: Cancer, Leo, Scorpio, Ophiuchus and Aquarius.

12th Assumption: *The Signs of the Zodiac are categorized as male or female:*
Male: Aries, Gemini, Leo, Libra, Sagittarius, Aquarius
Female: Taurus, Cancer, Virgo, Scorpio, Capricorn, Pisces

Response: There is no scientific evidence which proves or indicates this position, which is inspired by human nature and the incomplete scientific knowledge available to Claudius Ptolemy at the time. Therefore, it does not apply.

13th Assumption: *Each planet has at least one sign of the Zodiac as its own planetary house, where it is considered to reside "permanently". The houses of the planets are the following:*
Sun: Leo
Moon: Cancer
Saturn: Capricorn, Aquarius
Jupiter: Sagittarius, Pisces
Mars: Aries, Scorpio
Venus: Libra, Taurus
Mercury: Gemini, Virgo

Response: There is no scientific evidence to support this assumption. On the contrary the theories pertaining to the creation of the Solar System maintain that the creation of the planets was indeed a dynamic process that lasted a long time and in no way do they confirm the planets initial positions of residence as those postulated by Western Astrology.

14th Assumption: *The Signs of the Zodiac are divided into submissive and dominant. The summer (aestival) semi-cycle incor-*

porates the dominant and the winter (hyemal) semi-cycle the submissive.

Response: This assumption is inspired by the citizen-slave relationship in the time of Ptolemy. Such a transposition to the Zodiac circle today is completely inappropriate.

15th Assumption: *The Signs of the Zodiac are divided into equivalent or otherwise. Equivalent signs are those directly facing each other. They are known as equivalent because when one rises the other sets.*

Response: Today we are aware that the sky is not symmetrical and that the constellations of the Zodiac occupy irregular positions on the ecliptic. Therefore it is not possible to say that equivalent signs exist.

16th Assumption: *All zodiac constellations which do not have a relationship between each other of the above type are disjointed.*

Response: Quite correct.

17th Assumption: The Signs of the Zodiac have familial relationships between each other based on their specific positions:

First of all, those which are at a distance of 180° (degrees) (opposite) from each other are related; that is, for each pair of Zodiac constellations, there are 6 complementary relationships:
Aries-Libra
Taurus-Scorpio
Gemini-Sagittarius
Cancer-Capricorn
Leo-Aquarius
Virgo-Pisces
Secondly, those which are separated by 120° (degrees) – in a trian-

gular position or Trine - are said to be in harmonious aspect.
There are 4 Triplicities:
Aries-Leo-Sagittarius (rulers: the Sun by day and Jupiter by night)
Taurus-Virgo-Capricorn (rulers: Venus by day and the Moon by night)
Gemini-Libra-Aquarius (rulers: Saturn by day and Mercury by night)
Cancer-Scorpio-Pisces (rulers: Mars together with Venus by day and the Moon at night)
Thirdly, those forming a quartile are said to be in non-harmonious (tense) aspects, and fourthly, those forming a sextile, or hexagon, like the trine, are said to be in harmonious aspect.

Response: This position is without scientific foundation.

18th Assumption: *The constellation which is in ascendance in a specific location at the moment of a person's birth is known as the Ascendant, and is of great consequence for his/her character. On the basis of the Ascendant, the Houses of the Natal Horoscope are determined.*

Response: It is correct to refer to the constellation rising at the time of birth as the Ascendant. However, this can in no way be considered to have an impact on the person's character, due to the fact that the stars of each Zodiac constellation are tens or thousands of light years away from us.

19th Assumption: *Starting from the horoscopic ascendant, the 12 houses, considered to represent the various elements characterizing human existence, can be constructed.*

Response: A totally fallacious assumption, given that the concept of the Houses is based on constellations many light years away, which can have no influence over our personality.

20th Assumption: *The newly-discovered planets affect our horoscope in combination with those already known.*

Response: Yes, the new planets Uranus and Neptune will have an effect. Pluto and Chiron are not planets and do not exert the same influence.

2. Incorrect construction of the Horoscope

In the last chapter, we saw the step-by-step construction of the horoscope for Dimitris, who was born on 29/3/1980 at 13.00 in Athens. We have already explained how all of this is WRONG! More specifically, the following mistakes were made:

I. The construction of a circle with 12 equal subdivisions representing the 12 Signs of the Zodiac circle.

This is a mistake because, first of all, the scientific facts indicate that there are 13 Zodiac constellations on the ecliptic and, secondly, that the intervals between them are unequally distributed. For example, the arc length of the Zodiac Sign of Cancer is 20.1°, Leo is 35.8° and Scorpio is 6.6°. The 13th Zodiac constellation is Ophiuchus.

II. The positions of the Zodiac constellations on the ecliptic have changed since 100 A.D. when Claudius Ptolemy formulated his theory. Today, point "γ", at the intersection of the celestial equator (which is the extension of the Earth's equator in the celestial sphere) with the ecliptic (the path of the Sun in the sky), has changed position and is located in the constellation of Pisces.
The dates on which the Sun passes through the constellations of the Zodiac from 12/3/2012 to 12/3/2013 are shown in the following table (with the old, erroneous dates of Western Astrology in the first column.)
The complete annual tables through which you can find your true Zodiac sign are to be found in appendix 2 at the end of the book, and the details for all years can be found on the website:
www.astrology13.com

III. Absolutely all the positions of the planets are incorrectly shown in the charts-horoscopes of Western Astrology due to the shift of the Zodiac circle by more than 29.21° over the last 2094 years. For the sake of accurate calculation, this is calculated as follows: The shift of point "γ" is equivalent to approximately 29.21 days (the period from 21 March at 00:00, to 19 April at 6:00, time that the Sun passes to Aries in the year 2011). If we multiply the number of years that it takes point "γ" to move one degree, which is 71.71 years, by 29.21, this gives us a number equivalent to 2094 years. Therefore, Western Astrology is based on circumstances in about 83 B.C.

ZODIAC SIGN	**Western Astrology**	**13 Zodiac Sign Astrology From 12/3/12 to 12/3/13**
PISCES ♓	19/2-20/3	12/3, 00:20 – 18/4, 12:20
ARIES ♈	21/3-20/4	18/4, 12:20 – 13/5, 23:50
TAURUS ♉	21/4-21/5	13/5, 23:50 - 21/6, 7:10
GEMINI ♊	22/5-21/6	21/6, 7:10 – 20/7, 12:00
CANCER ♋	22/6-22/7	20/7, 12:00 – 10/8, 11:10
LEO ♌	23/7-23/8	10/8, 11:10 – 16/9, 12:20
VIRGO ♍	24/8-22/9	16/9 12:20 – 31/10, 00:40
LIBRA ♎	23/9-23/10	31/10, 00:40 - 23/11, 3:20
SCORPIO ♏	24/10-22/11	23/11, 3:20 – 29/11, 15:30
OPHIUCHUS Φ		29/11, 15:30 – 17/12, 23:00
SAGITTARIUS ♐	23/11-21/12	17/12, 23:00 – 19/1, 18:10
CAPRICORN ♑	22/12-20/01	19/01, 18:10 – 16/2, 4:50
AQUARIUS ♒	21/1-18/2	16/2, 4:50 - 12/03, 06:20

Table showing the dates on which the Sun passes through the Zodiac constellations, according to Western Astrology and 13 Zodiac Sign Astrology.

The wrong Natal Horoscope

How can astrological predictions be made when:

a. The Zodiac star sign is incorrect (e.g. due to displacement it is Pisces rather than Aries in Dimitri's case)

b. The Ascendant is incorrect (Cancer rather than Leo)

c. The Houses which are determined at 30° intervals in an anti-clockwise direction starting from the Ascendant, are also incorrect.

d. The positions of the planets are incorrectly identified. (Mercury is in Aquarius and not Pisces, Venus is in Aries and not Taurus, Jupiter is in Leo and not Virgo, Saturn is in Leo and not Virgo, the Moon is in Leo and not Virgo, Uranus is in Libra and not Scorpio, Neptune is in Ophiuchus, not Sagittarius. Mars is in Leo, however, its position within the correct constellation in this case being successfully determined only by a few degrees.

e. Lastly, the astrological tables-almanacs convert reality to fantasy. They transport the positions of the Zodiac constellations, the Ascendant, the Houses and the planets precisely **2094 years back into the past.**

3. The false concept of the Ascendant which is alleged to influence our lives

The concept of the Ascendant, that is, the Zodiac constellation which is rising at the moment of a person's birth, is an anachronism. We cannot say in the year 2011 that a constellation in which the stars are tens or thousands of light years away can directly affect our lives. For example, in Dimitris' case, the As-

cendant ascribed to him by Western Astrology is Leo. The visible stars in the constellation of Leo are:
Star α-Leonis : It is known as Basiliscos (the Greek variant) (Regulus in Latin), and is 85 light years away.
Star β-Leonis : Known as Denebola. 42 light years away.
Star γ-Leonis: 100 light years away.
Star δ-Leonis: 52 light years away.
Star ε-Leonis: 310 light years away.
Star ζ-Leonis: 120 light years away, this has a visual double.

The light which reaches us today from α-Leonis was emitted from it in 1926 (exactly 85 years ago). Does anyone really believe that α-Leonis can exert an influence over our lives?

Let us not be naïve. It is just not possible! People may have believed this in the Middle Ages, but now we know that this simply cannot be. The Sun, the Moon and the planets might influence us, but stars at a distance of tens and hundreds of light years away cannot.

For this reason, Astrology must directly adapt. We will see in detail in Chapter 3 of Part 2 that our only real Ascendant is the Moon. It is next to us, it exerts a pull on us; it creates tides and eclipses, has phases and oscillations, affects animals, plants, our psychology and love life, and is responsible for many other phenomena which we are still in the process of discovering. Careful study will show that only the Moon can be our Ascendant.

PART 2

THE ASTROLOGY OF THE THIRTEEN SIGNS OF THE ZODIAC

Chapter 1

Assumptions and theoretical foundations

a. New Assumptions

There is a solution to the anachronistic delusions of the old Astrology. In order to examine this in more detail we must start from the basic principles of the New Astrology of the 13 Signs of the Zodiac.

1. It has been known for centuries that matter is not composed of fire, water, earth and air! This is also true of its main manifestations, which are not heat, dryness, moistness and cold. That is what Ptolemy believed in 100 A.D. Since then, science has made great leaps. We shall take as the foundation of the new Astrology, in terms of the composition of matter, that which is accepted by modern science: **molecules** and **atoms**, **photons** (waves),

leptons and **quarks**. In the place of the manifestations we have the 4 fundamental interactions of matter and energy: **gravitation**, **electromagnetism**, and **weak** and **strong** interactions. The first is responsible for the movement of planets, the second for the electrical forces and magnetic fields in nature, while the third and fourth control interactions in the world of atoms and their nuclei.

2. The planets of our Solar System, our Sun and Moon have an impact on our lives in a variety of ways. The Sun has the greatest impact. Its energy is absolutely essential for our survival. Without the Sun, there is no life.
3. The Moon is in turn the second most influential celestial body. Full moons, tides, eclipses and the phases of the Moon have a major impact on us and our planet. The Earth's satellite is justifiably the new Ascendant. It is not a planet, but it is proven to affect our lives more than any other celestial body, with the exception of the Sun.
4. Venus, Mars, Jupiter and Saturn have a lesser effect due to their distance. They assume equilibrium within the system. Uranus and Neptune constitute the remainder of the planets, given that Pluto is not considered to be a planet because it does not fulfill the criteria of the IAU (International Astronomical Union). The planets, through their magnetic fields, affect the Earth – Moon system and by extension our lives. It is not impossible that other influential objects or forces may be discovered in the future.
5. The 13 constellations of the Zodiac on the ecliptic, that is, the path of the Sun as it moves across the sky, are considered, in modern Astrology, to act as identifiers of the position of the Sun at different seasons of the year rather than stars which influence our lives.

6. We will introduce and establish a new astrological variable which greatly affects our lives: the number of **sunspots**. This varies over an 11 year period from approximately 0 to 200 (there could be more, of course). When the Sun is going through an intensely active phase with many sunspots, then this can have a strong impact on all of us. The effects of the electromagnetic storms there can be felt on Earth, with many phenomena, including the Aurora Borealis (the Northern Lights) and disturbances in the Earth's magnetic field, among others.
7. The planets cannot be considered to reside permanently in a particular constellation of the Zodiac as was formerly the case under older systems. Here we take the moment of birth as our starting point. This determines, for each one of us, the properties associated with the residence of each planet, the Sun and the Moon.
8. The aspects, i.e. the trines, quartiles, oppositions and conjunctions of the planets, are also applicable when adapted to the 13 Zodiac Sign system. We will examine all of this in more detail in subsequent chapters.
9. The position of point "γ" is adjusted by 50.2" of a degree per year, exactly as science indicates.
10. General characteristics can be attributed to the planets, which were falsely ascribed by the old Astrology to the Houses. More specifically, the Moon can be seen to affect financial affairs and associations, and Mercury travel and education. Venus affects relationships, primarily romantic ones. Mars represents limitations and enmity, and Jupiter the home and family. Saturn is associated with death and sex. Uranus is associated with friends and Neptune with career, work and health.

From the above, it is clear that we are dealing with a new Astrology, which is not as simple and symmetrical as the old one.

The number 13 is an odd number, a prime number in mathematics. But since nature and convention have indicated this interpretation, this is what we shall work with. In any case, the Moon revolves around our Earth 13 times a year, and the constellation of Ophiuchus has been known to exist for 2,500 years now.

The New Astrology is asymmetrical and demands new data in order for it to be studied. Fortunately there are computers which can make the calculation of the new Ascendant and our predictions easier.

The New Astrology of the 13 Signs is much simpler than the old one because we have abandoned the old Ascendant which we proved to be false. This cannot affect our lives as Western Astrologers claim. In its place comes the Ascendant we call the Moon. It affects our lives every day, even more so on the day we were born.

b. The Signs of the Zodiac

The Signs of the Zodiac can no longer be categorized, as they were under the old premises, into:

1. fire, air, earth and water
2. male and female
3. impulsive, fixed and bicorporeal
4. fixed planetary houses
5. dominant and submissive.

They have certain attributes which stem from their positions on the ecliptic. That is, the Sun and the planets confer certain attributes rather than the other way around.

c. The theoretical background of the New Astrology

The British Astronomer Percy Seymour, in his book *Astrology: The Evidence of Science*, supports the idea that organic life responds through its neural networks to the magnetic properties of the Earth, the Moon and the planets. Thus he states that the magnetic field of the Earth vibrates at a wide range of natural frequencies and that the tidal forces of the planets are capable of making these natural frequencies and keep pace with them. Human beings respond to certain of these oscillating frequencies. Seymour goes on to say: "The orbits of the planets cause changes in the Earth's magnetic field". Disturbances in the magnetic field affect the developing foetus as it becomes attuned to the resonances. The frequencies to which the foetus is tuned remain the same throughout its life. In his latter book, published in 1997 under the title The Scientific Basis of Astrology: Tuning to the Music of the Planets, Percy Seymour further develops his theory.

He says accordingly that all scientists now accept that solar activity affects the magnetic field of the Earth through solar wind. He also says that the Moon affects the upper atmosphere through its tidal forces, creating electrical currents which in turn affect the magnetic field of the Moon itself. It is also proven that the magnetic field of the Earth is used by living organisms, including humans, for orientation and the timing of their biological cycles.

There are indications, says Seymour, that the positions and movement of the planets in relation to the Sun play a significant role in solar activity. There are also indications, (which are the subject of violent dispute) that particular planetary positions can, at the moment of birth and not only then, affect a person's character. Seymour's theory suggests that the outer planets, Jupiter, Saturn, Uranus and Neptune, affect the flow of currents within the Sun which in turn determine the Sun's magnetic field. This occurs primarily via the influence they exert over the center of mass of our Solar System.

The Sun's magnetic field and solar wind in turn cause fluctuations in the Earth's magnetic field. Thus we see that ultimately the planets regulate the changes in the Earth's magnetic field through the Sun. Another important contribution of the planets, according to Seymour, is the tuning and locking of certain frequencies of the Earth's magnetic field to the rhythm of the planets, through their gravitational interaction with the gases trapped by the Earth's magnetosphere. The harmonic oscillations produced by the Earth's magnetic field are captured by the neural network of the foetus in the womb and synchronize the biological clock which determines the date of birth.

The distinguished Astrophysicist also says that the tuning of the magnetic "antenna" of the foetus by the above vibrations also determines which genes will be activated and impart individual characteristics.

The French psychologist and statistician Michel Gauquelin (1928-1991) carried out statistical research into the effect of the planets on people's lives. The first of these research studies concerned 508 eminent French doctors. He found that the majority of them had been born with Mars or Saturn rising or at the Midheaven[7].

Another study of 570 French champion athletes revealed that Mars was rising or at the Midheaven at the time of birth of 355 of them.

---

7 Michel Gauquelin, "Astrology and Science"

Another of his studies was of 25,000 parents and their children, where he found that the sky at the time of birth of the children was quite similar to that at the time of birth of their parents.

Therefore, New Astrology uses scientific research and natural interactions for its documentation. This is the only acceptable way for the establishment and development of astrology in modern times. It is obvious that a new frame is required to incorporate the work and research of Dr. Michel Gauquelin and Dr. Percy Seymour. Astrology of the 13 signs of the Zodiac aspires to make a step in that direction.

Chapter 2

The SUN, our life

The star which gives us life is huge. Its diameter is 1,392,000 km. Its mass is approximately 2,000,000,000,000,-000,000,000,000,000,000 kilos. Its average surface temperature is 5,500 degrees Celsius.

In the context of our galaxy, however, it is a very small star producing energy through the fusion of hydrogen in its core. A proton – proton (p-p) chain reaction converts hydrogen to helium in its core at a temperature of 15,000,000 degrees Celsius. This chain releases energy in the form of gamma rays and neutrinos. Each second 700,000,000 tons of hydrogen are converted into 695,000,000 tons of helium and the remaining 5,000,000 to energy in the form of gamma rays. The Sun consists of 70% hydrogen, 28% helium and 2% heavy metals. The stocks of hydrogen are sufficient for another 5 billion years. Almost all the energy we use on earth is directly or indirectly provided by the Sun.

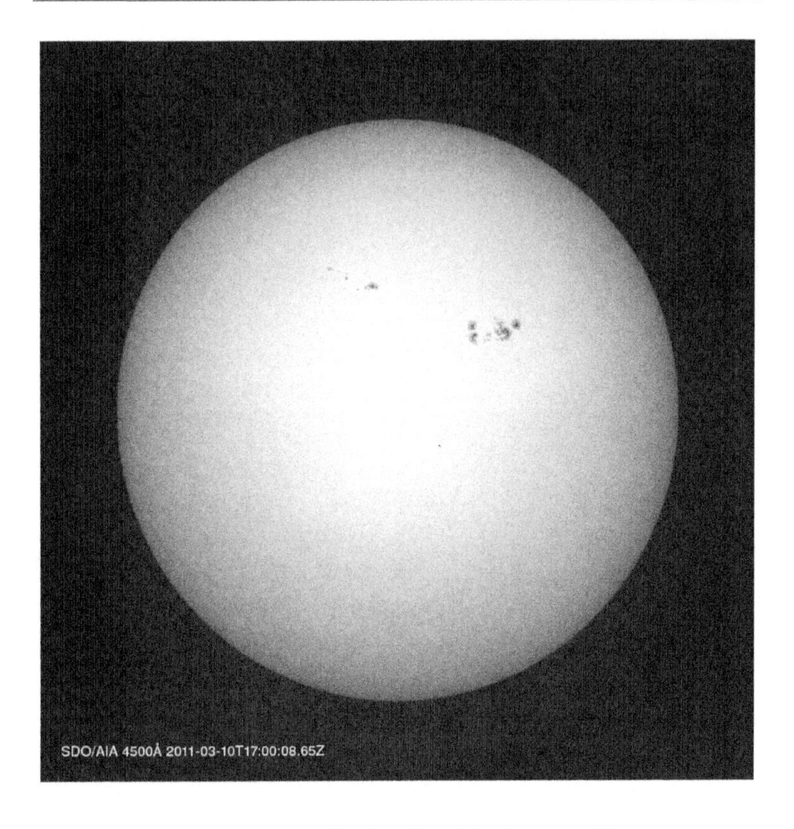

Figure 2.2-1: The Sun (NASA photograph)

Hydrocarbons (oil, natural gas), the water cycle, wind power and biological energy all owe their existence to our Sun.

All living creatures and plants on our planet also owe their existence to the Sun, as do human beings, who are, as entities, very much affected by it.

The human clock is synchronized to the Sun. Sleeping, waking and work are programmed to the daily movement of the Sun. People's psychology is profoundly affected by our star. According to research, those who live in more northern latitudes with less sunlight suffer more from depression and are more pessimistic. In terms of a person's psychology, being born in spring and being born during winter months can have different consequences.

The Sun warms us and helps to metabolize vitamins in the body.

The Sun takes on a central role in the New Astrology. Its position on the ecliptic gives us our zodiac sign, which forms the crucial part of our predictions. Many of our characteristics can be seen to arise from the position of the Sun at the time of birth.

The Sun in a Zodiac constellation exerts its influence through the season, the distance and the angle at which it emits its rays towards the Earth.

The Sun symbolizes power, light, courage, rebirth, the whole of things.

Chapter 3

The Moon, the New Ascendant

1. Natural characteristics

The Moon is Earth's only natural satellite. From space the Earth-Moon system appears to be a double planet. The Moon has a diameter of 3,476 km and its average distance from Earth is 385,000 km. Every 27.3 days the Moon completes one full orbit around the Earth with respect to a fixed point in space (a sidereal month). Because of the simultaneous movement of the earth around the sun, the moon needs 29.5 days to go from full Moon to full Moon (a synodic month). The difference between the synodic and the sidereal month is shown clearly in figure 2.3-1.

We always see the Moon from the same side because its revolution is synchronized with its rotation. That is, it takes 27.3

days to rotate around its axis, exactly as long as it takes to complete its revolution around the Earth. The moon's orbit plane is inclined to the ecliptic by about 5° (degrees), and its rotation axis is inclined at a 1.5° (degree) angle to its orbit.

Thus 6.5° (degrees) are visible beyond the North and South poles of the Moon. This phenomenon is known as libration in latitude.

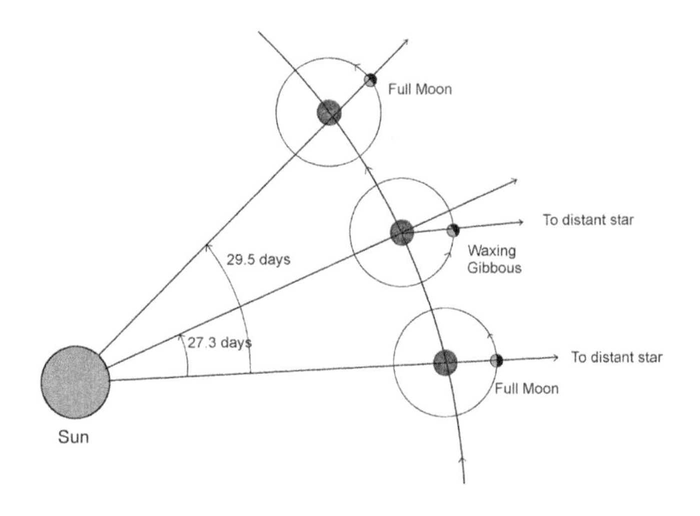

Figure 2.3-1: Interpretation of the Synodic (29.5 days) and the Sidereal (27.3 days) Months. Design by V. Kanatas.

Apart from the impressive phenomenon of its phases, which is due to the monthly movement of the triple celestial system of Sun – Earth – Moon, the Moon also arrests us with other phenomena:

- The eclipses of the Sun and the Moon which are due to the alignment of the triple system: Sun – Earth – Moon. The greatest number of eclipses per year is 7 and the minimum is 2.
- The tides of the sea and large lakes on Earth, which are largely due to the effects of the Moon (and also the Sun).

One of the main features of the Moon is its stabilizing effect on the orbit of the Earth.

Figure 2.3-2: The Moon (Source: NASA)

Research shows that the sexual reproductive cycles of sea urchins in the Red Sea and polychaete Eunice sea-worms in the Pacific Ocean, follow the lunar month. The same apparently applies to the level of activity of rats in a dark room which fluctuates according to the position of the Moon.[8]

But could it also be possible, that the sexual life and reproduction of humans is regulated by the Moon? We know that the menstrual cycle coincides with the average of the sidereal month (27.3 days) and the synodic month (29.5 days). Is this totally random? In nature and the process of evolution, nothing can be considered completely random. Are there any more concrete examples of the influence of a celestial body on our lives?

2. The Moon as Ascendant

Today we know that the ascendance of a particular zodiac constellation at the time of birth of a child has an insignificant influence on them. The constellations which correspond to the Ascendant are comprised of stars at a distance of from 10 to 3000 light years away. The same applies to the Midheaven (MC), the Nadir (IC) and the Descendant (Desc) of the zodiac constellation at a person's time of birth.

The calculations which traditional Astrologers make with reverence and precision, are totally meaningless. The dependence of the Ascendant on the meridian and the latitude is a fallacy. For latitudes north of 66.5° N and south of 66.5°S, the Ascendant cannot with equal probability be in one of the 12 old Signs of the Zodiac, and this is because there is a problem with

8 Gauquelin, "Astronomy and Science"

their ascendance. The further north in the sky the zodiac constellation determining the ascendant is, the lower the possibility of it rising in the most northern latitudes.

Thus, at 70°, only 8 zodiac constellations can be ascendant in Western Astrology. Imagine the problems this causes for anyone born at latitudes more than 66.5° N to the north[9].

The word "horoscope", derives etymologically from the Greek words "Ora" (ora = hour) and "skopos" (skopo = observe). In Astrology it has the meaning of observing something at the time of the birth of a baby. In Western Astrology, the "Horoscope" in the Greek sense is translated as "Ascendant" in English, that is, the Zodiac constellation which is rising in the East at a person's time of birth. The Horoscope as an observation of the phenomena at the moment of birth may, as we shall show below to be the case, ultimately turn out to be something more than the Ascendant.

Our Horoscope in the modern age is, as we shall see, independent of the geographic position of a person's birth. The position of the Moon on the ecliptic is independent of our latitude and longitude, and by extension independent of the place of birth of each person. Therefore the appropriate indicator possibly pointing to the personality of each person is the exact position of the Moon on the ecliptic (at their time of birth). This is our Horoscope, our Ascendant. Just as the Moon stabilizes the Earth's orbit, so is our character regulated by it.

Thus, the Moon represents our ego, our character. It defines our relationships in life, our constitution, our finances and our relationships with siblings and family.

---

9 Read more in the book by Ronny Martens and Tim Trachet, *Making Sense of Astrology*.

Given its clear relationship with the tides of the seas, rivers and lakes, we can theorize that the Moon governs all things related to the water element.

Chapter 4

The elevated contemporary role of the planets

In an earlier chapter we examined the views of the British astronomer and astrophysicist, Percy Seymour, who suggests that the Earth's magnetic field vibrates with a wide range of natural frequencies. He also emphasizes that the tidal forces of the planets are capable of tuning these natural frequencies so that they harmonize with them, and that human beings respond to certain frequencies of vibration. Let's examine the main physical characteristics of the planets as well as their inner symbolism as these are perceived by Astrology.

Figure 2.4-1: The Sun and the Planets (Source: NASA)

MERCURY

The closest planet to the Sun and the smallest in our Solar System. It is visible from Earth at dawn and twilight due to its short distance from the Sun [maximum elongation (angular distance) 28° degrees].

It has a diameter of 4,878 km and has an average distance from the Sun of 58,000,000 km. It completes one full orbit around the sun in 88 days and has a sidereal rotation period of 58.6 days. The length of the day on Mercury is equivalent to 87.5 Earth days.

Figure 2.4-2: Mercury (Source: NASA)

Due to its close proximity to the Sun, surface temperatures reach up to 430° Celsius during the day and -170° Celsius at night. Due to the fact that the Sun attracts comets and asteroids, Mercury, as the closest planet to it, is a target for these celestial bodies. Its surface is covered with impact craters created by past asteroid collisions.

Symbolism:
Mesopotamia: Messenger, rainmaker, successor.
Claudius Ptolemy: Alternately drying and absorbing moisture or a bringer of moisture.
Under the 13 Signs of the Zodiac: Communication, emotion, travel, information, intellect. It determines travel and education.

VENUS

Venus is similar to Earth in mass and size. It has a diameter of 12,100 km and its average distance from the Sun is 108,000,000 km. Its maximum elongation (angular distance) is 48° (degrees), which results in it being visible only up to 3 hours before sunrise (the "Morning Star") or three hours after sunset (the "Evening Star"). Venus displays phases, like the Moon, which were discovered by Galileo using his telescope. It is covered by clouds, its orbital period is 225 days and it takes 243 days for it to rotate about its axis. It rotates from west to east, in the opposite direction to that of the Sun.

Figure 2.4-3: Venus (Source: NASA)

The atmosphere of Venus consists of 96% carbon dioxide, 3% nitrogen, and other gases. It has a surface temperature of 482 degrees Celsius, due to the greenhouse effect created by the clouds of carbon dioxide which prevent ground radiation from escaping into space. If it had a thin atmosphere without cloud cover its surface temperature would only be 60 degrees Celsius. The surface of Venus is swept by winds of up to 360 km/hour.

Symbolism:

Mesopotamia: Fertility, peace, reconciliation.

Claudius Ptolemy: Has creative powers of a temperate nature. It is moderately warming, but it mostly brings moisture.

Under the 13 Signs of the Zodiac: Balance, sex, love, passion, femininity, beauty, sociability. It defines human relationships, mainly sexual ones.

MARS

The so-called red planet, due to its reddish appearance. It has a diameter of 6,800 km and a distance from the Sun of 228,000,000 km. It rotates about its axis in 24 hours and 28 minutes, and its orbital period is 687 Earth days. The atmosphere on Mars consists of 95.32% carbon dioxide, 2.7% nitrogen and 1.6% argon; its atmospheric pressure is equivalent to 1/100 of that on Earth.

Figure 2.4-4: Mars (Source: NASA)

In 1877, A. Hall discovered the two satellite moons of Mars, Deimos and Phobos. Their diameters are 15 and 27 km respectively.

Symbolism:

Mesopotamia: Lord of Death, Hell and the heat of the summer.
Claudius Ptolemy: The nature of Mars is to dry and to burn.
Under the 13 Signs of the Zodiac: Conflict, hatred, war, enmity, determination, action, aggression, self-preservation, energy, power. It defines our limitations and our enemies.

JUPITER

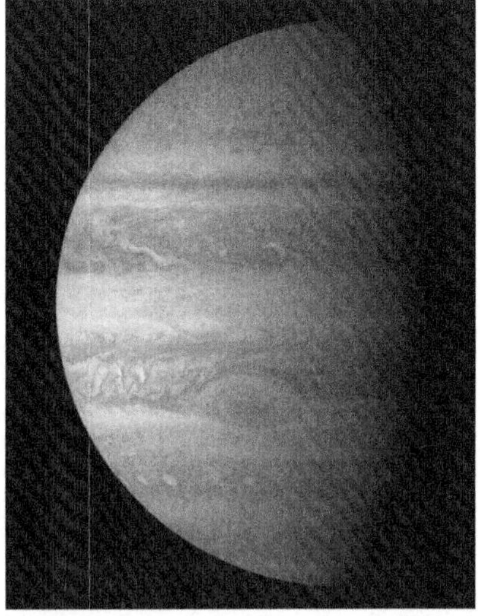

Figure 2.4-5: Jupiter (Source : NASA)

The largest planet of our Solar System; it has a diameter of 143,000 km and an average distance from the Sun of 778,000,000 km. It is a gas giant planet consisting of 75% hydrogen and 25% helium.

The upper atmosphere is visibly segregated into zones

along its latitude and storms rage among them. One of these storms is the Great Red Spot which has been in existence since at least the time of Galileo and is more than three times the size of Earth. Jupiter takes 12 years to complete an orbit around the Sun and rotates about its axis in 10 hours on the equator. It has rings like Saturn, but they are not visible from Earth.

Jupiter has at least 63 natural satellites. The four brightest of these were discovered by Galileo in 1610: Io, Europa, Ganymede, Callisto. These four have the greatest diameters, from 2,880 to 4,980 km. Jupiter has a very powerful magnetic field; at 4.2 Gauss it is approximately 14 times more powerful than that of the Earth. Jupiter's magnetosphere extends to a distance greater than 150 million km, depending on the pressure of the solar wind. Many accelerated particles from Jupiter's magnetosphere reach as far as the Earth. There are also belts of radiation (Van Allen type) and an aurora effect similar to the Aurora Borealis on Earth.

Symbolism:

Mesopotamia: A beneficial influence, peacemaker

Claudius Ptolemy: Has temperate creative powers, a beneficial influence.

Under the 13 Signs of the Zodiac: Creative power, governance of emotions, optimism, good fortune, faith, philosophy, hope, vision, plenty. It defines the home, family, and children.

SATURN

Another gas giant, with a diameter of 120,660 km, the second largest after Jupiter. It takes 30 Earth years to finish one revolution around the Sun, and rotates about its axis in 10 hours and 14 minutes. Its average distance from the Sun is 1.4 billion km. It has nine rings, which consist of particles of dust and ice. It also has 62 natural satellites, not counting the smaller ones. Titan, the largest moon of Saturn, has a dense atmosphere.

The atmosphere of Saturn consists mainly of hydrogen (96.3%) and helium (3.25%). There are also very small quantities of methane, ethane, acetylene and ammonia.

Figure 2.4-6: Saturn (Source: NASA)

It has an intrinsic magnetic field which reaches an intensity of 0.2 Gauss at the equator. Saturn is the only planet in the solar system that is less dense than water. While the core has a density greater than water, its outer part is so thin that its overall specific density is $0.69gr/cm^3$ ($<1gr/cm^3$).

Symbolism:
Mesopotamia: A beneficial influence, bringer of stability and prosperity.
Claudius Ptolemy: It cools and dries; a maleficent planet.
Under the 13 Signs of the Zodiac: Negative influence, development, restrictions, limits, endurance, discipline, denial, cruelty. It defines deeper feelings, symbolizes death and also sex.

URANUS

Uranus is the third largest planet in our Solar System. It has a rocky core, similar in size to that of Earth, surrounded by a layer of water and ammonia. The atmosphere of the planet consists of hydrogen, helium and methane.

Its rotational axis lies almost on the ecliptic. Its satellites and its rings rotate perpendicular to its equator. Because of this, each pole has a period of night and a period of day, equivalent to 21 Earth years. As a consequence, the planet's magnetosphere lies in the opposite direction from the Sun.

It takes 84 Earth years to complete one revolution around the Sun and 17.9 hours to rotate about its axis. Its minimum distance from Earth is 2.57 billion km and its distance from the Sun is 2.87 billion km.

Symbolism:
It was not known to the peoples of Mesopotamia or Ancient Greece since it was only discovered by William Herschel in 1721.
Under the 13 Signs of the Zodiac: Revolution, evolution, intuition, transformation, liberation. It determines friends.

Figure 2.4-7: The planet Uranus (Source: NASA)

NEPTUNE

Neptune is the eighth and farthest planet from the Sun in our Solar System. It is a gas giant with a diameter of 49,500 km and an average distance from the Sun of 4,500 million km. It has two natural satellites, Triton and Nereid.

It is similar in composition to Uranus, and both differ from Jupiter and Saturn. The atmosphere of Neptune is similar to that of Jupiter and Saturn in that it is composed primarily of hydrogen and helium, whilst it contains a higher percentage of water, ammonia and methane.

Figure 2.4-8: Neptune (Source: NASA)

Astronomers place Uranus and Neptune in the category of "ice giants" The inner core of Neptune, like Uranus, is mainly composed of rock and ice. Traces of methane in the inner atmosphere of the planet are what give it its blue appearance. Neptune's magnetic field has a strange orientation. Its axis forms an angle of about 50° degrees relative to the rotational axis of the planet. The center is approximately 13,500 km from the physical center of Neptune (offset by 0.55 radii). The reason for this extreme discrepancy is not yet known. The intensity of the magnetic field is roughly equivalent to 1/5 of the intensity of the Earth's magnetic field. This magnetic field may be generated by movements of conductive materials (perhaps a combination of ammonia, methane and water) in its middle layers.

Symbolism:

It was not known to the peoples of Mesopotamia or Ancient Greece because it was discovered as recently as 1821 by Alexis Bouvard, and was first observed by Johann Gottfried Galle based on the calculations of Urbain Le Verrier.

Under the 13 Signs of the Zodiac: Imagination, ecstasy, romance. It determines health, work, and career.

PLUTO

According to Astronomers, as of 2006, by decision of the IAU (International Astronomical Union), our Solar System has 8 planets, as well as a number of dwarf planets. Pluto belongs to the dwarf planets due to its small mass. Other dwarf planets are the asteroids Ceres and Eris.

Pluto has a diameter of 2,300 km, that is, smaller than that of the Moon. It is at a distance of 5,900 million kilometres from the Sun and its orbit intersects that of Neptune, but because it is highly inclined (17.2° degrees) relative to the ecliptic there is no danger of collision. The closest that the two planets can come to each other is 500 million km. Its small size and proximity to Neptune suggest that it may be an escaped satellite.

Chapter 5

Ophiuchus and the New Zodiac

The characteristics which the signs of the zodiac confer on each person are related to the following parameters.

1. The position of the Sun on its ecliptic orbit. The ecliptic orbit is essentially the abstract projection of the Earth's orbit which considers the Sun to revolve around the Earth!
2. The season of the year.
3. The individual properties of the orbit.

All of these are reflected in the person and affect their life and character. If a person is born in spring, when the Sun climbs high on the ecliptic, they will tend to be happier and more optimistic than a person born in the heart of winter.

Because of the precession of the equinoxes, many of the

characteristics attributed to the old signs of the zodiac have moved. When a new sign of the zodiac occupies an arc length on the ecliptic which represents part of two or more signs under the old zodiac, then the corresponding profile is constructed based on the principle of proportionality and the external traits peculiar to the new sign.

Let us look, for example, at Virgo, which occupies a 44° degree arc length on the ecliptic. If we look at figure 2-1 in Chapter 2 of Part 1, we can see that Virgo will take on 100% of the characteristics of Libra, about 20% of the characteristics of Virgo under the old system, and lastly, 25% of the characteristics of the old Scorpio. All of this arises from the figure and is self-explanatory.

It is necessary here to mention that the signs of the zodiac can be considered to exert an overall influence to the extent that they are host to the Sun, the Moon and the planets. With the help of the images below, we shall take a look at the constellations of the zodiac and discuss their stars.

In the time of Hipparchus, the stars were classified on a scale of apparent magnitude from 1 to 6 according to their brightness. The brightest of these were assigned a value of 1 and the fainter they became, the further they moved up the scale, as far as 6. Today, the data has been expanded and we have widened the scale to include values less than 1, i.e. 0, -1, -2 for bright stars of greater intensity. Using a telescope, we can see very faint stars with an apparent magnitude of over 24. Each value is 2.5 fainter than the previous one. Thus, a star with an apparent magnitude of 1 is 2.5 times brighter than one with a magnitude of 2.

Ascend. No.	Name	Constellation	Apparent Magnitude	Range Type	Brightness (Sun = 1)	Distance (light years)
1	Sirius	Canis Major	-1,46	A1	26	8,7
2	Canopus	Carina	-0,72	F0	15000	310,0
3	Alpha Centauri	Centaurus	-0,04	G2	1,7	4,3
4	Arcturus	Boötis	0,00	K2	115	36,0
5	Vega	Lyra	0,03	A0	52	25,0
6	Capella	Auriga	0,08	G8 F0	90 - 70	43,0
7	Rigel	Orion	0,12	B8	60000	910,0
8	Procyon	Canis Minor	0,38	F5	7	11,4
9	Achernar	Eridanus	0,46	B5	400	85,0
10	Betelgeux	Orion	0,0 – 0,9	M2	105000	640,0
11	Agena	Centaurus	0,61	B1	10000	460,0
12	Altair	Aquila	0,77	A7	10	16,6
13	Acrux	Crux Australis	0,83	B1	3200	360,0
14	Aldebaran	Taurus	0,85	K5	120	68,0
15	Antares	Scorpius	0,96	M1	7500	330,0
16	Spica	Virgo	0,98	B1	2100	260,0
17	Pollux	Gemini	1,14	K0	60	36,0
18	Fomalhaut	Piscis Australis	1,16	A3	13	22,0
19	Deneb	Cygnus	1,25	A2	70000	1550,0
20	Becrux	Crux Australis	1,25	B0	8200	425,0

Table showing the 20 brightest stars in the sky

Carina	Dorado	Libra	Pictor	Triangulum Australe
Cassiopeia	Draco	Lupus	Pisces	Tucana
Centaurus	Equuleus	Lynx	Pisces Austrinus	Ursa Major
Cepheus	Eridanus	Lyra	Puppis	Ursa Minor
Cetus	Fornax	Mensa	Pyxis	Vela
Chamaleon	Gemini	Microscopium	Reticulum	Virgo
Circinus	Grus	Monoceros	Sagitta	Volans
Columba	Hercules	Musca	Sagittarius	Vulpecula
Coma Berenices	Horologium	Norma	Scorpius	
Corona Australis	Hydra	Octans	Sculptor	
Corona Borealis	Hydrus	Ophiucus	Scutum	
Corvus	Indus	Orion	Serpens	
Crater	Lacerta	Pavo	Sextans	
Crux	Leo	Pegasus	Taurus	
Cygnus	Leo Minor	Perseus	Telescopium	
Delphinus	Lepus	Phoenix	Triangulum	

List of the 88 constellations

PISCES ♓

Sun in Pisces from March 12, 00:20 to April 18, 2012, 12:20

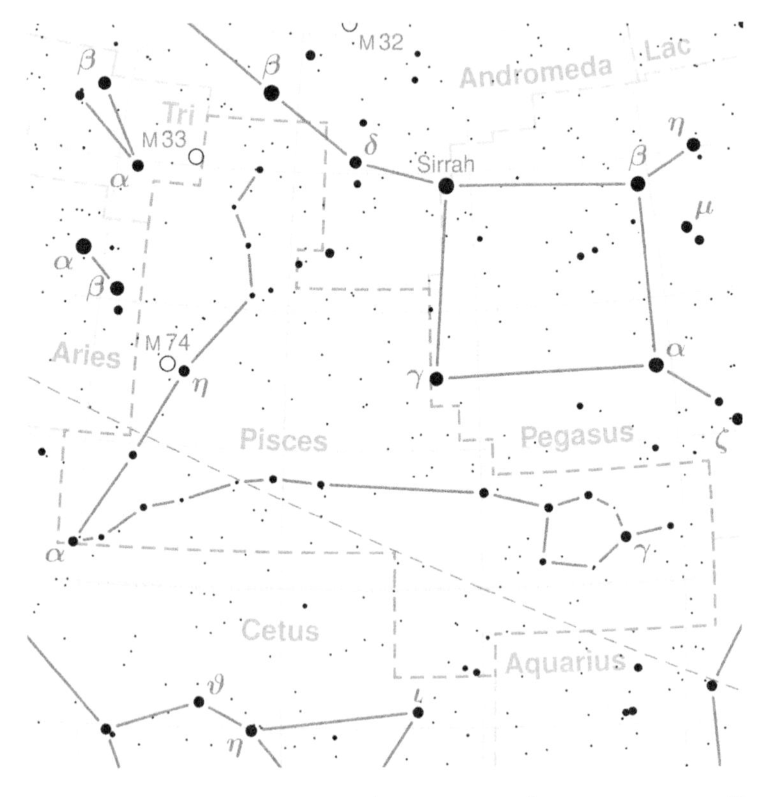

Figure 2.5-1: The Constellation of Pisces. Image by Torsten Bronger[10]

10 Copyright © 2003 Torsten Bronger. Published with permission of the author. The same applies to all images of the constellations published in the following pages.

> "Beyond Aries and a little to the south is Pisces. One higher than the other, thus to hear the north wind blow stronger"
>
> (Aratus of Soli, *Phaenomena*)

From a mythological point of view, Pisces represents the transformation into a fish of the goddess Aphrodite and her son, Eros, who jumped into the Euphrates River to escape the giant, Typhon.

Star α-Piscium: Al Rischa. Double star with magnitudes of 4.3 and 5.2, located 98 light years away.
Star β-Piscium: Fum al Samakah, or 'mouth of the fish'. Magnitude 3.5, 320 light years away.
Star γ-Piscium: Magnitude 3.7, 160 light years away.
The section of the ecliptic which is in Pisces has an arc length of 37°.

Basic characteristic: The beginning.
Primary characteristics: Self-expression, worry, dynamism, impatience, initiative, courage, aggression, impulsiveness, passion, selfishness, leadership tendencies, self-obsession, self-preservation, confusion, and escape.

ARIES ♈

Sun in Aries from April 18, 12:20 to May 13, 2012, 23:50

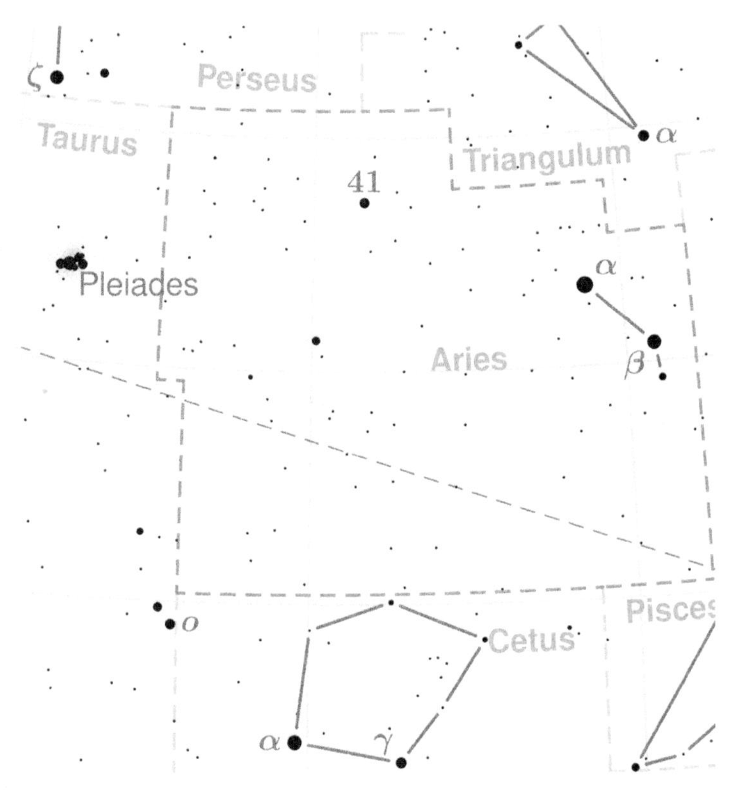

Figure 2.5-2: The Constellation of Aries is the old ruler of the zodiac circle.

The second constellation of the zodiac on the ecliptic. Western Astrologers consider it to be the first zodiac sign. Aries in the heavens represents the golden-fleeced ram of Greek mythology.

The children Phrixus and Helle escaped, on a ram, from Athama and their step-mother Ino, who wanted to sacrifice them to the gods. The unfortunate Helle fell off the ram into the Dardanelles Strait while the children were flying towards the city of Aia (Colchis). Because of this, the strait was named the Hellespont. Phrixus reached Aia alone, where he sacrificed the ram to Zeus and gave its fleece to King Aietes. Later, Jason organized the Argonaut campaign, managing to take back the Golden Fleece and return it to Greece.

Star α-Arietis: Hamal, that is, "ram" in Arabic. It has an apparent magnitude of 2.0 and is 85 light years away.
Star β-Arietis: Sheratan. The star marked point "γ" in the time of Hipparchus. It is 46 light years away and has an apparent magnitude of 2.6.
Star γ-Arietis: Mesharthim. A binary star with magnitudes of 4.75 and 4.83, 160 light years away.
The section of the ecliptic which is in Aries has an arc length of 24.8°.

Basic characteristic: Stability.
Primary characteristics: Strength, materialism, productiveness, a practical mind, security, sensuality, stubbornness, possessiveness, routine, and patience.

TAURUS ♉

Sun in Taurus from May 13, 23:50 to June 21, 2012, 7:10

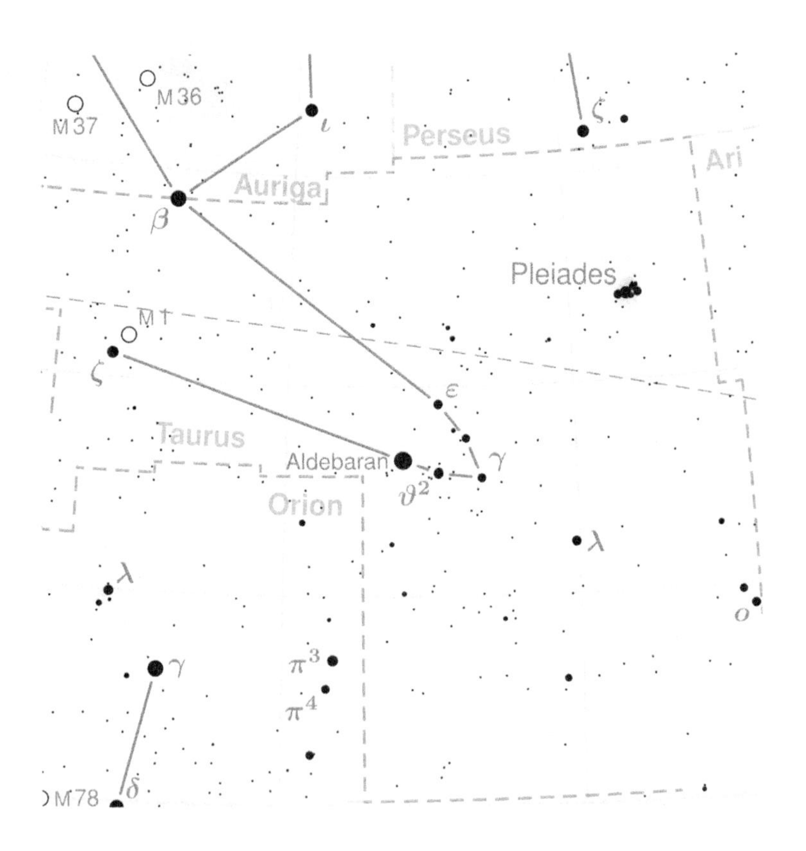

Figure 2.5-3: The Constellation of Taurus

A phantasmagorical constellation, rich in stars visible to the naked eye, with the bright red Aldebaran, as well as one of the most spectacular star clusters in the sky, the much sung Pleiades. Taurus held the position of the first constellation of the zodiac circle from 4000 to 1700 B.C., but lost it due to the precession of the equinoxes, as we analyzed earlier.

The myth of Zeus, who transformed himself into a bull in order to deceive the beautiful Europa, gave this constellation its name. Zeus managed to marry Europa in the cave of Dicti on Crete.

Star α-Tauri: Aldebaran, who follows the Pleiades. A red giant with a magnitude of 0.9, 68 light years away.
Star β-Tauri : El Nath. A blue giant with a magnitude of 1.7, located 140 light years away.
Star ζ-Tauri: Magnitude 3.0, 490 light years away.
The section of the ecliptic which is in Taurus has an arc length of 36.7°.

Basic characteristic: Adaptability:
The main characteristics of Taurus are: Communication, duality, diplomacy, eloquence, curiosity, socializing, intellect, duplicity, multi-facetedness, worry, symmetry, stubbornness, the desire to have a good time, and sluggishness.

GEMINI ♊

Sun in Gemini from June 21, 7:10 to July 20, 2012, 12:00

Castor and Pollux were the twins, lauded and loved, who became a constellation so that mortals would remember them. This is the fourth zodiac constellation.

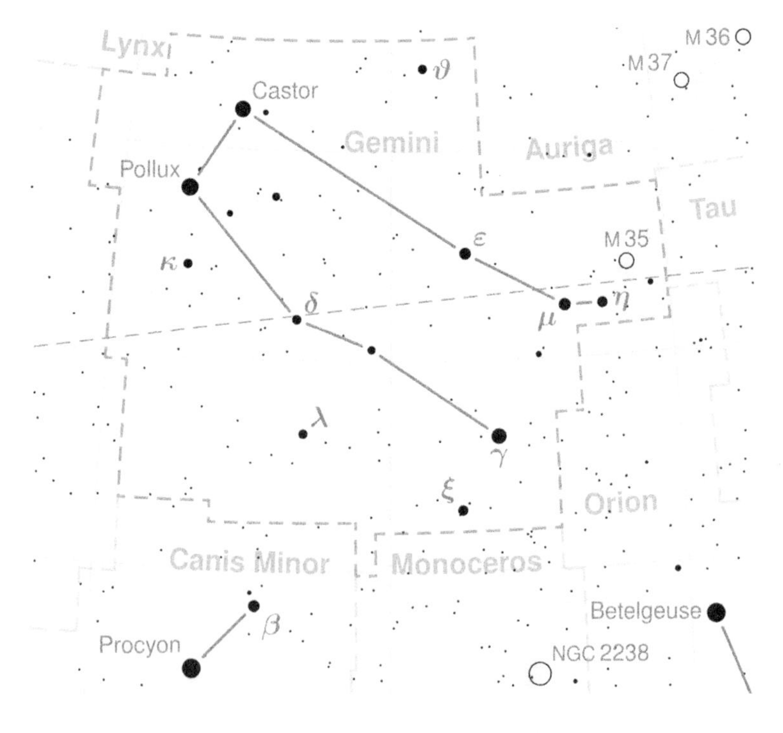

Figure 2.5-4: Castor (α) and Pollux (β) – the Twins (Gemini)

They were sons of the god Zeus and Leda – thus they were known as the Dioskouri [Dios (Zeus), Kouroi (children)]. They were also brothers of Helen of Troy and Clytemnestra. They became famous in the ancient world for their deeds and their participation in the Argonaut's quest. However, what made them immortal was their inseparable brotherly love and friendship. When, after many adventures, Pollux looked down on his dead brother's face, he asked his father, Zeus, to kill him so that he could once again go to meet his brother in Hades. Zeus told him to choose: either to live forever among the Gods of Olympus, or to live alternately one day in Hades with his brother, and one day on Olympus. Pollux chose their common fate in the dark and the light.

Star α-Geminorum: Its name, Castor, comes from ancient Greece. It is a multiple star, with a magnitude of 1.6, and is to be found 45 light years away.
Star β-Geminorum: Pollux. Magnitude 1.1, 36 light years away.
Star γ-Geminorum: Alhena. Magnitude 1.9, 85 light years away.
The section of the ecliptic in Gemini occupies an arc length of 27.8°.

Basic characteristic: Sensitivity.
The main characteristics of Gemini are: Motherhood, emotion, sensitivity, protection, compassion, ambition, temperamental, tenderness, embrace, insecurity, nostalgia, and manipulation.

CANCER ♋

Sun in Cancer from July 20, 12:00 to August 10, 2012, 11:10

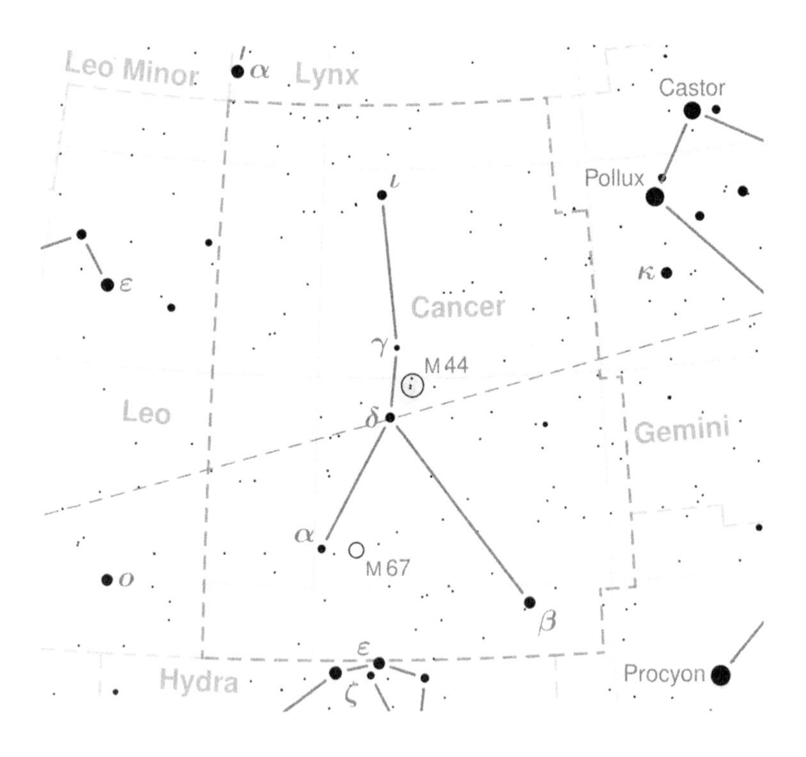

Figure 2.5-5: The Constellation of Cancer.

Cancer, or the Crab, according to Greek mythology, helped the Lernaean Hydra in the battle against Hercules. During the duel Cancer harassed the hero by biting his legs.
Hercules crushed the Crab with his foot and then killed the Lernaean Hydra. The goddess Hera raised Cancer to the heavens in order to reward him for his trust and friendship.

In the time of Claudius Ptolemy, Cancer was in the summer solstice, the farthest angular distance of the Sun from the celestial equator (23.5° degrees). Today, this point is in the Constellation of Taurus, due to the precession of the equinoxes (the movement of point «γ», the point of intersection of the celestial equator with the ecliptic, by 50.2" seconds of a degree per year).

Star α-Cancri: Acubens, which means 'claws' in Latin. It has a magnitude of 4.3 and is 100 light years away.
Star β-Cancri: Al Tarf, or "the end", due to its position to the bottom right of the constellation. It has a magnitude of 3.5, and is 170 light years away.
Star γ-Cancri: Asellus Borealis, Latin for "northern donkey colt". Magnitude 4.7, 200 light years away.
The section of the ecliptic in Cancer has an arc length of 20.1°.

Basic characteristic: Enthusiasm.
The main characteristics of Cancer are: Strength, pride, confidence, generosity, noisiness, drama, and resilience.

LEO ♌

Sun in Leo from August 10, 11:10 to September 16, 2012, 12:20

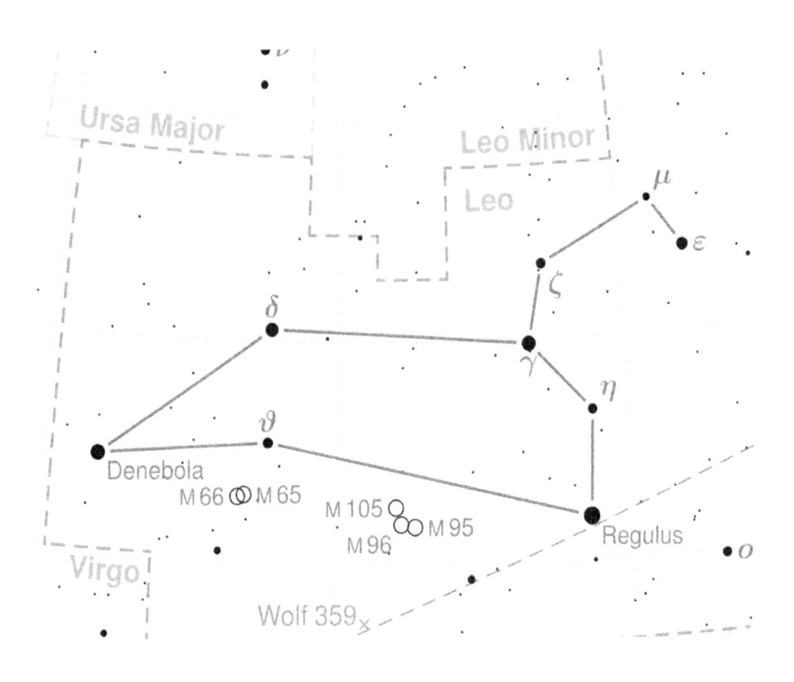

Figure 2.5-6: The Constellation of Leo. Basiliscos (Regulus) touches the ecliptic.

The constellation which represents the Nemean Lion killed by Hercules in the first of his labors. It is located in the northern hemisphere of the sky, and the imaginary lines between its stars form a lion.

The constellation borders Ursa Major and Leo Minor to the north, Sextans and Crater to the south, Virgo and Coma Berenices to the east, and Cancer to the west.

Star α-Leonis or Basiliscos, (Regulus in Latin). It has an apparent magnitude of 1.4, and is 85 light years away. It is almost on the ecliptic.
Star β-Leonis: Denebola, the tail of the lion. It has an apparent magnitude of 2.1 and is 42 light years away.
Star γ-Leonis: Algieda. A double star with magnitudes of 2.3 and 3.5, 100 light years away.
The section of the ecliptic contained in Leo has an arc length of 35.8°.

Basic characteristic: Competence.
The main characteristics of Leo are: Service, discretion, analysis, perfectionism, conscientiousness, originality, fertility, submissiveness, humility, righteousness, pomposity, and authoritativeness.

VIRGO ♍

Sun in Virgo from September 16, 12:20 to October 31, 2012, 00:40

The constellation is very large, covering 1294 square degrees in the sky. The stars α, ζ, δ, γ, and θ form a visible pentagonal shape in the sky.

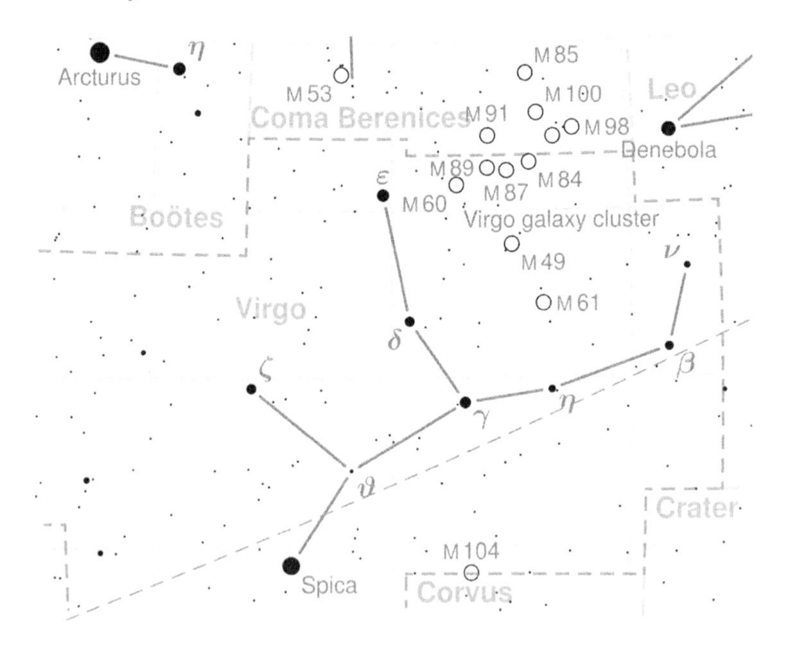

Figure 2.5-7: Virgo. Contains point γ' symmetrical to point γ on the ecliptic.

According to mythology, Virgo is identified with Persephone, the daughter of Demeter and Zeus. Persephone was abducted by Hades (Pluto), God of the Underworld, who made her his wife. Demeter, in her anger, commanded that no flower should bloom and no tree bear fruit. With the intervention of Zeus, an agreement was reached, by which Persephone had to spend six months of the year in Hades, (Hades is the name of the underworld kingdom, as well as its ruler) and the other six months of the year with the gods on Olympus. Thus, we have 6 months of autumn and winter, when the earth is dormant, and the other 6 months when Persephone is in the Overworld, when the earth is fertile, and we have spring and summer.

Star α-Virginis: Spica. This is an ecliptic double star whose magnitude changes by 0.1 every 4 days. It has an apparent magnitude of 1.0 and is 260 light years away.
Star β-Virginis: Zavijava. A yellow star with a magnitude of 3.6, 33 light years away.
Star γ-Virginis: Porrima. A double star with a magnitude of 2.8. It is 36 light years away.
The section of the ecliptic which is contained in Virgo has an arc length of 44°.

Basic characteristic: Harmony.
The main characteristics of Virgo are:
Selectivity, narrow-mindedness, peaceful relationships, companionship, cooperation, diplomacy, perfectionism, indecision, crisis, adaptability, aesthetics, trauma, hatred, revenge, and self-destruction.

LIBRA ♎

Sun in Libra from October 31, 00:40 to November 23, 2012, 3:20

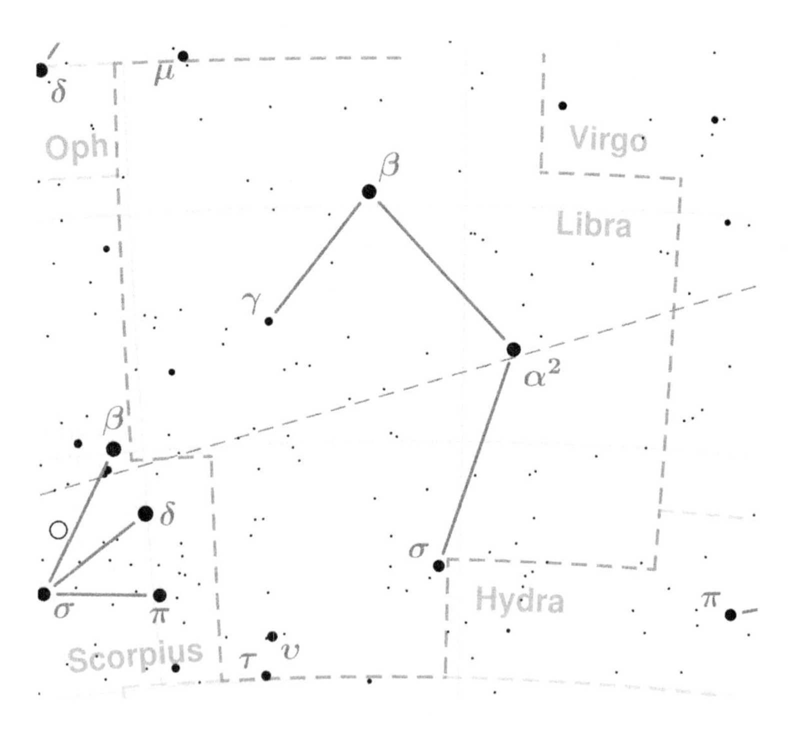

Figure 2.5-8: Libra was at one time an extension of Scorpio, its claws, which is apparent from the figure.

It is the 8th zodiac constellation and used to contain the second point of intersection of the ecliptic with the celestial equator. Today this point is in Virgo.

The ancients called it Chelae Scorpionis, or 'the claws of Scorpio'. From the age of Hipparchus (2nd century B.C.), it took the name Libra. It is the only sign which is represented by an inanimate object (the Scales). Its name comes from its old position on the ecliptic, when it divided the sky in half.

Star α-Librae: Zubenelgenubi. A double star, the parts of which are visible to the naked eye. It has magnitudes of 2.8 and 5.2 and is 72 light years away. It is tangential to the ecliptic.
Star β-Librae: Zubenelschamali. It has a greenish colour, a magnitude of 2.6 and is 120 light years away.
Star γ-Librae: Zubenelacrab. It has a magnitude of 3.9 and is 75 light years away.
The section of the ecliptic which is contained in Libra has an arc length of 23.2°.

Basic characteristic: Intuition.
The main characteristics of Libra are: Mutability, tension, magnetism, power, skill, sex, secrets, destruction, mystery, and suspicion.

SCORPIO

Sun in Scorpio from November 23 3:20 to November 29, 2012, 15:30

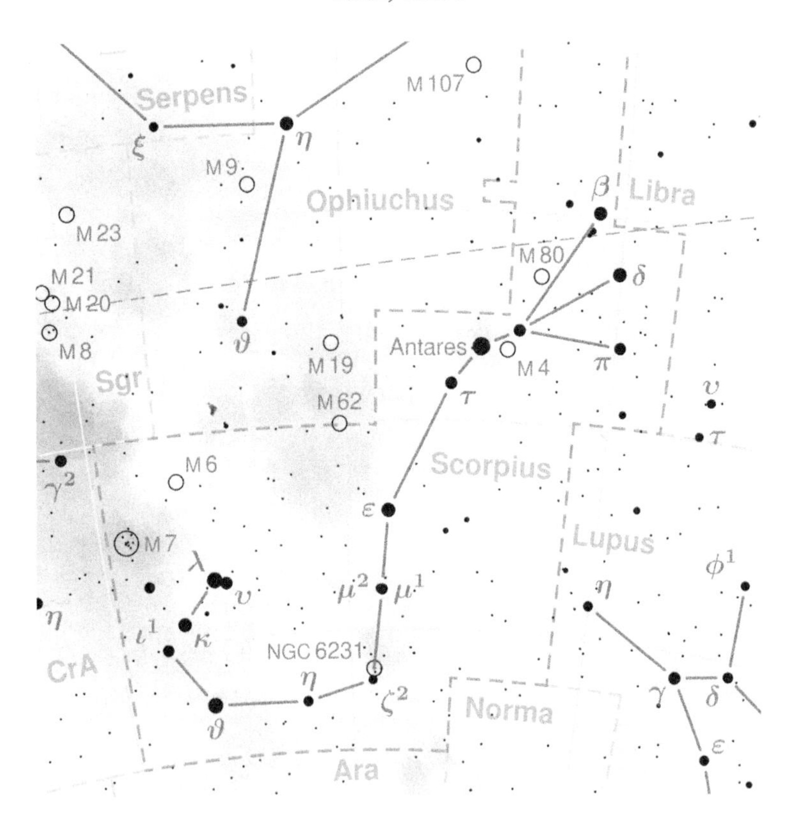

Figure 2.5-9: Scorpio, with Antares.

This is the only constellation whose shape is remarkably similar to the animal of the zodiac sign it represents. The stars ε, μ, ζ, η, θ, ι, κ, λ make up its tail and its sting, whilst τ, α, σ, π, δ, β, ω comprise the front part of its head.

According to mythology, Scorpio was sent by mother Earth to kill the hero Orion because, as a hunter, he was killing the animals which inhabited the Earth. Scorpio finally managed to kill Orion and both were elevated to the stars to become constellations.

α-Sco is known as Antares (that is, "anti-ares", Ares being Mars) because the ancient Greeks often confused it with the planet Mars due to its reddish colour. Today, the course of the Sun through the constellation is just 6.6° degrees, i.e. about 6 days, from the 23rd to the 30th of November. The result is that very few people are born under this sign!

Star α-Sco: Antares. A red supergiant star, with an apparent magnitude which changes from 0.9 to 1.1 every 5 years. It is about 600 light years away.
Star β-Sco: Graffias. A double star with magnitudes of 2.6 and 4.9, 540 light years away.
Star δ-Sco: Dschubba. A blue-white star with a magnitude of 2.3, 550 light years away.
The section of the ecliptic in Scorpio has an arc length of 6.6° degrees.

Basic characteristic: Extrovertedness.
The main characteristics of Scorpio are: Indifference, fun, free thinking, extravagance, and worry.

OPHIUCHUS Φ

Sun in Ophiuchus from November 29, 15:30 to December 17, 2012, 23:00

Ophiuchus lies between the constellations of Hercules and Scorpio, and the head of Serpens as far as its tail. Its southern part lies within the galactic plane.

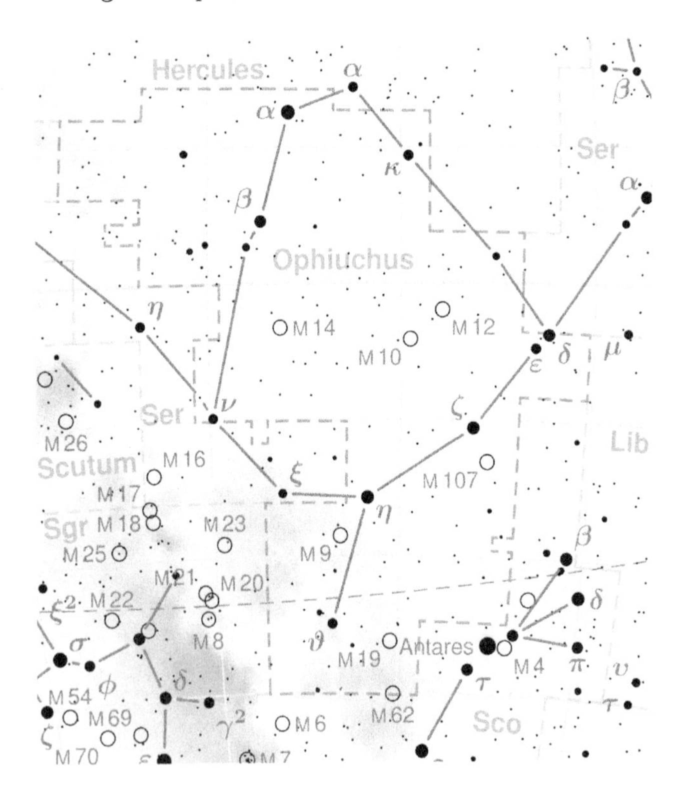

Figure 2.5-10: The much discussed constellation of Ophiuchus.

According to mythology, Ophiuchus is identified with Asclepius, the renowned physician of antiquity. The close association between Asclepius and the snake is due to the fact that snakes represented wisdom, rejuvenation, and the power of the discovery of new healing herbs.

Asclepius was educated and received instruction from his father Apollo and the centaur Chiron; he was the first doctor and served in the Argonaut campaign in this capacity. When he returned from the journey he was even considered capable of raising the dead.

The cases of Hyppolytus and Orpheus are well known among those he attempted to bring back to life. The King of Hades was so troubled by his behaviour that he asked Zeus to punish him. Thus Zeus killed the first doctor of the human race with a lightning bolt. The father of Ophiuchus, Apollo, made him immortal, raising him to the heavens as a constellation.

Star α-Ophiuchi: Ras Alhague, the head of Ophiuchus. It has a magnitude of 2.1 and is 62 light years away.
Star β-Ophiuchi: Gebalrai, the heart of Ophiuchus. A yellow giant with a magnitude of 2.8, 120 light years away.
Star γ-Ophiuchi: It has a magnitude of 3.8 and is 115 light years away.
The section of the ecliptic which is in Ophiuchus has an arc length of 18.6°.

Basic characteristic: Challenge.
The main characteristics of Ophiuchus are: Searching, curiosity, adventure, spontaneity, optimism, ambition, and freedom.

SAGITTARIUS ♐

Sun in Sagittarius from December 17, 23:00, 2012 to January 19, 2013, 18:10

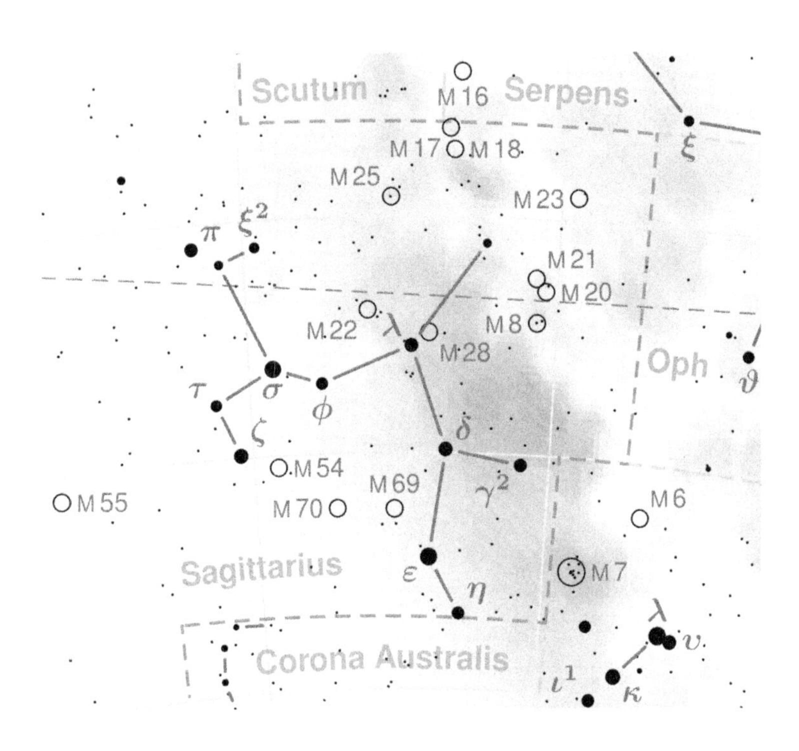

Figure 2.5-11: The Constellation of Sagittarius.

It lies in the southern hemisphere of the sky and borders on Ophiuchus, Scorpio, the Corona Australis, the Microscope and Capricorn.

It is the 11th constellation of the zodiac circle and in recent years the Sun has been passing through it from 18th December to 20th January.

According to mythology, Sagittarius represents the centaur Chiron, teacher to Ophiuchus. In the celestial charts of the Middle Ages, Sagittarius is represented with an arrow pointing at Scorpio.

Star α-Sagittarii: Rukbat, or 'the knee of the archer, Sagittarius'. It has a magnitude of 4.0 and is 200 light years away.
Star β-Sagittarii: Arkab Prior and Arkab Posterior, a double star with magnitudes of 3.9 and 4.3, 220 and 130 light years away, respectively.
Star γ-Sagittarii: Al Nasl, the point of the archer's arrow. It has a magnitude of 3.0 and is 120 light years away.
The section of the ecliptic which is in Sagittarius has an arc length of 33.4°.

Basic characteristic: Responsibility.
The main characteristics of Sagittarius are: Conservatism, stability, power, authoritarianism, discipline, prudence, self-restraint, sense of duty, cohesion, pessimism, toughness, patience, conventionality, narrow-mindedness, and idealism.

CAPRICORN ♑

Sun in Capricorn from January 19, 18:10 to February 16, 2013, 4:50

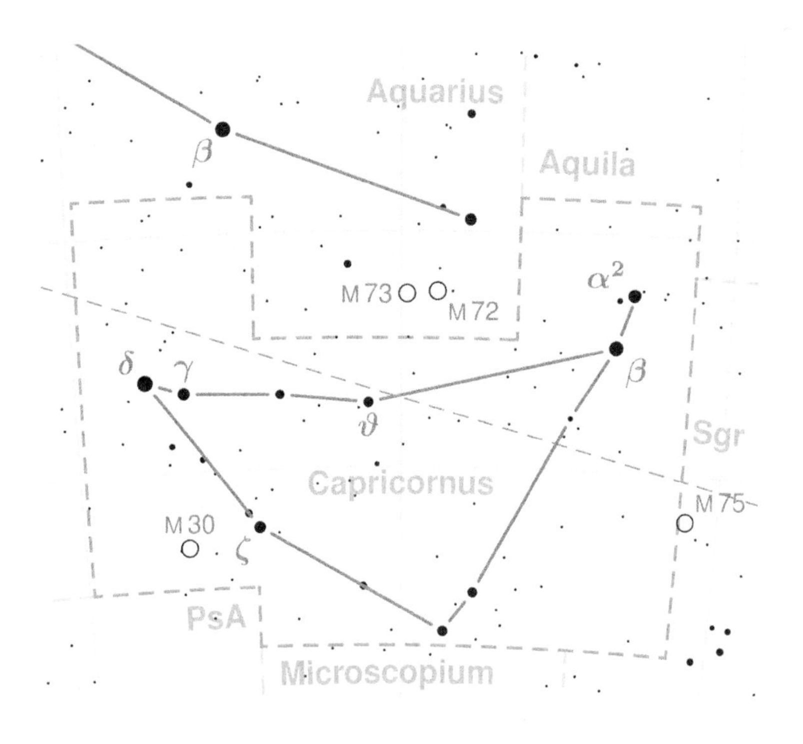

Figure 2.5-12: The Constellation of Capricorn.

According to the prevailing mythological version, Capricorn symbolizes the Goat Amalthea, whose milk fed Zeus when he was a baby. When Amalthea died, Zeus wished to honour her, thus making her a constellation so that she would remain immortal in the sky.

Aratos of Soli was the first to call the Constellation Capricorn, so as to distinguish it from the star Capella (little goat) in the constellation of the Charioteer, Auriga. According to Eratosthenes, the constellation was known as Pan or Pan the Goat. The platonic philosophers thought that the souls of man rose to the skies through Capricorn. Because of this, the constellation was called the "Portal of the Gods".

Star α-Capricorni: Algiedi. A multiple star. It is a double star with magnitudes of 4.2 and 3.6, 1,600 and 120 light years away, respectively. Each of these two stars is also a double star.
Star β-Capricorni: Dahib, with a magnitude of 3.1, 250 light years away.
Star γ-Capricorni: Nashira, with a magnitude of 3.7, 100 light years away.
The section of the ecliptic which is in Capricorn has an arc length of 27.8°.

Basic characteristic: Idealism.
The main characteristics of Capricorn are: Altruism, detachment, coldness, revolution, reformation, justification, eccentricity, idealism, fraternity, objectivity, progressiveness, science, and unpredictability.

AQUARIUS ♒

Sun in Aquarius from February 16, 4:50 to March 12, 2013, 6:20

One of the most ancient constellations of the zodiac, the origins of which are lost in the mists of time. The constellation is represented in stone carvings of the ancient Babylonians as a man pouring water from a pitcher. The ancient Egyptians called him “Ku-ur-ku” and “Ramman” (Storm God), because when the Sun was in Aquarius the flooding of the Nile reached its highest point.

In Greek mythology, Aquarius represents Ganymede, the son of Tros and Callirrhoe. Zeus brought him to Olympus to make wine and nectar for the Gods, without taking into account the jealousy of the goddess Hebe, who was their wine maker. In order to resolve the problem, Zeus raised Ganymede to the skies, making him a constellation.

The most clearly visible part of Aquarius is the Y shape formed by the stars η, ζ, π, γ (in Aquarius), from which we can construct the entire ancient figure. Aquarius is the representation of a man pouring water from a pitcher towards the constellation of Piscis Austrinus.

In approximately 600 years, point “γ” on the ecliptic will reach the boundaries of the constellation. This will be the dawning of the Age of Aquarius.

Star α-Aquarii: Sadalmelic, or “the Luck of the King”. It has a magnitude of 3.0, and is 950 light years away. It is located on the celestial equator.

Star β-Aquarii: Sadalsuud, the “luck of lucks”, the luckiest star in the sky. It has a magnitude of 2.9 and is 980 light years away.

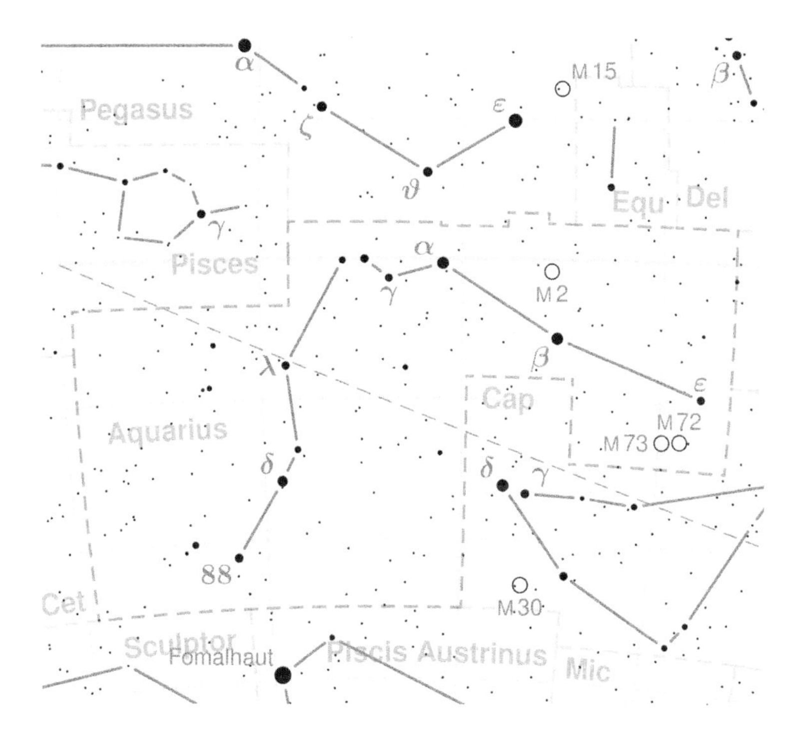

Figure 2.5-13: The Constellation of Aquarius.

Star γ-Aquarii: Sadaschbia. It has a magnitude of 3.8 and is 91 light years away.
The section of the ecliptic which is in Aquarius has an arc length of 24.2°.

Basic characteristic: Imagination.
The main characteristics of Aquarius are: Compassion, expressiveness, mysticism, day-dreaming, hesitation, and receptiveness.

Chapter 6

The aspects of the planets

Our guide to the interactions which occur when planets form certain angles (which Astrologers call the aspects) within the chart of our solar system, lies in the symmetries of the celestial bodies.

Figure 2.6-1: The Planets (Source: NASA – a collage)

When two planets are in orbit around the sun, we do not say that there are conditions of stability, but conditions of symmetry. Thus, their opposition, i.e. when they are facing each other, is a condition of symmetry, which is a positive event from an astrological point of view.

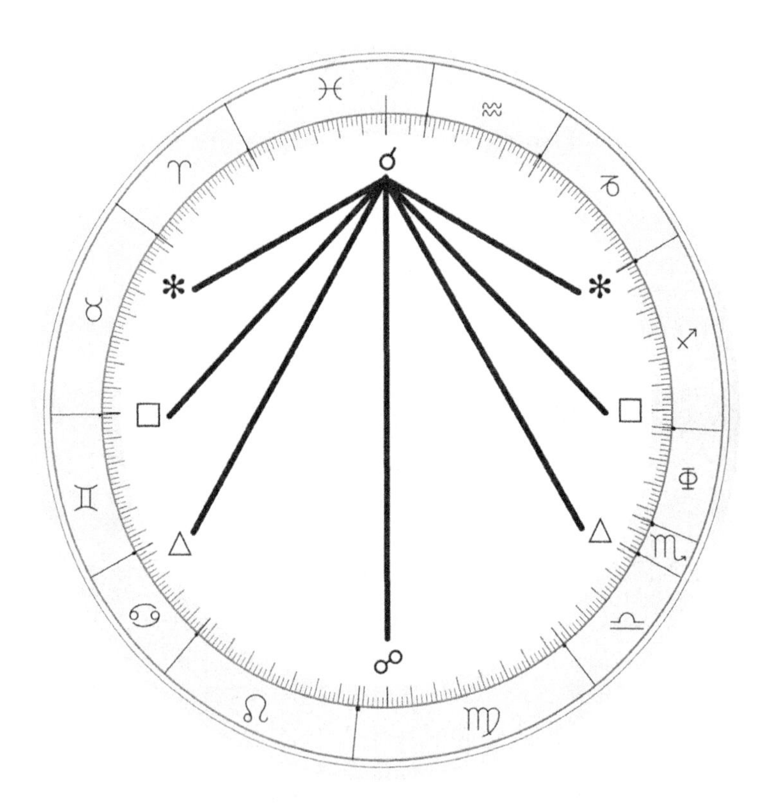

Figure 2.6-2: The aspects of the planets. The positions of the Zodiac Constellations are independent of the aspects.

By the same reasoning, wherever there is a conjunction, there is asymmetry, and as such, a negative event from an astrological point of view. The formation of a 60° angle between the three planets (even including the Sun or the Moon) functions as a dynamic balance in nature and for this reason we consider that the symmetry is positive, with positive astrological repercussions. The same applies to the formation of quartiles and sextiles between celestial bodies in our solar system, i.e. we have symmetry with positive astrological connotations.

To summarize:

The planets, Sun and Moon in a trine △ implies a dynamic balance, a positive event.

The planets, Sun and Moon in opposition ☍ implies a positive event.

The planets, Sun and Moon in conjunction ☌ implies conflicting characteristics, a negative event.

The planets, Sun and Moon in a quartile □ implies a dynamic balance, a positive event.

The planets, Sun and Moon in a sextile ⚹ implies a dynamic balance, a positive event.

In figure 2.6-2, we can see the planetary aspects recognized under the Astrology of the 13 Signs of the Zodiac.

When we have, for example, a planet in a 12 o'clock position then we say each planet in a 60° position is in a sextile ⚹, at 90° in a quartile □, at 120 ° or 240 ° in a trine △, and at 180° in opposition ☍.

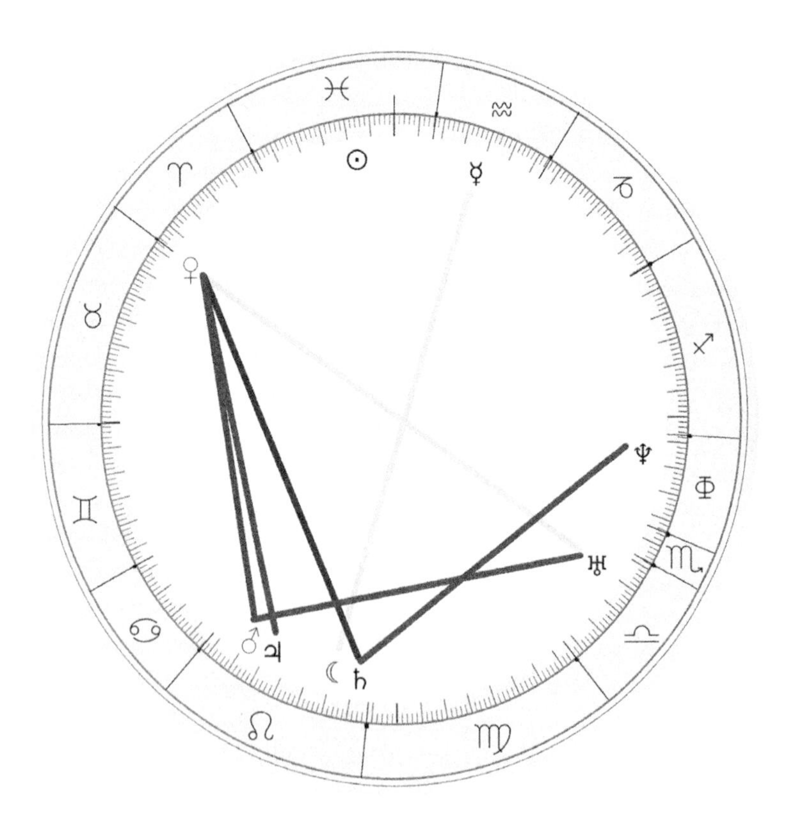

Figure 2.6-3: Dimitris' natal horoscope showing the aspects.

When a planet is within a distance of up to 8°, we say that it is in conjunction. For all of the angles described above, we accept a degree of elasticity of up to 8° (6° in the case of sextiles). In figure 2.6-3, depicted in red, we can see the quartile of Mars to Uranus and Mars to Venus.

Saturn is also in a quartile with Neptune, and Jupiter with Venus. In a trine position (blue) is Saturn with Venus. In opposition, in grey, we can see the Moon with Mercury and Uranus with Venus.

A prediction for the sample case of Dimitris, based on the aspects of the planets, will be developed in Chapter 8 of Part 2.

Chapter 7

A New Variable in Astrology: Sunspots

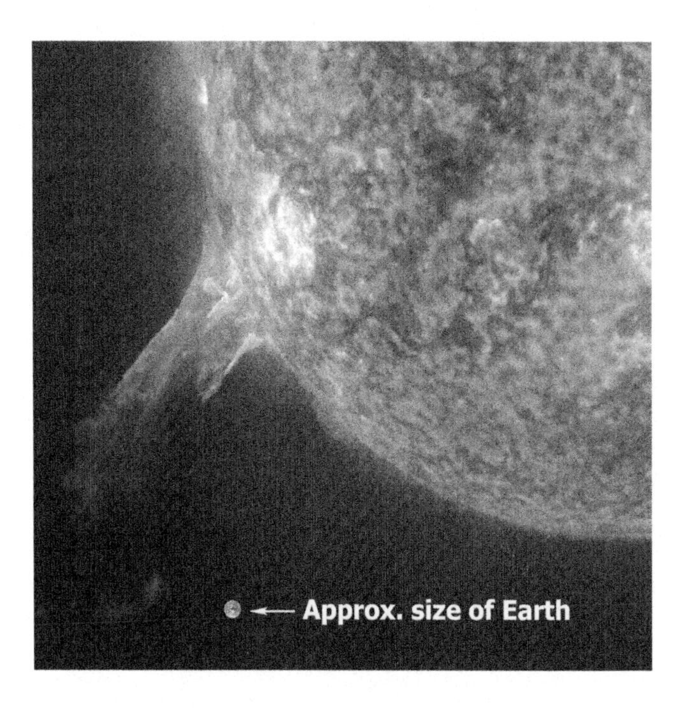

Figure 2.7-1: Part of the Sun compared to the size of Earth (Source: EISA/ NASA/SOHO)

1. What are sunspots?

Sunspots are black areas on the surface of the Sun. The reason they appear to be black is their much lower temperature, approximately 3,850 degrees Celsius, by comparison with the photosphere which surrounds them, where the temperature reaches 5,500 degrees Celsius. Sunspots were first observed by Galileo with his telescope in 1610. Their dimensions may exceed 100,000 km in diameter (the diameter of Earth is only 12,700 km) and have the following characteristics:

- **The umbra**: the black central area.
- **The penumbra**: the lighter zone around the umbra.
- **The filaments**: observed within the penumbra radiating towards the center of the umbra.

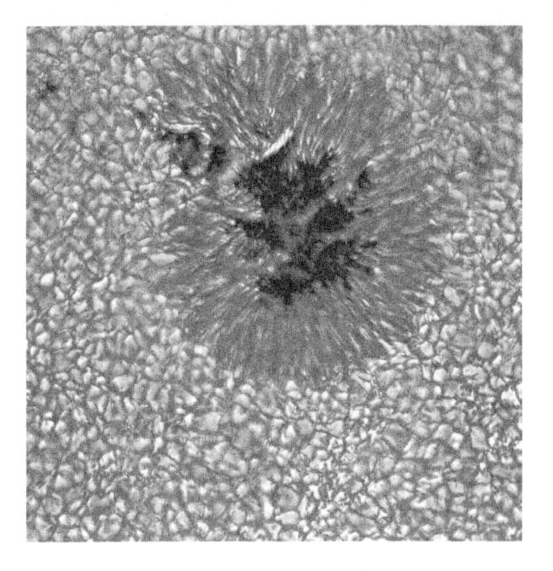

Figure 2.7-2: Magnified sunspot (Source: NASA).

Sunspots begin as a group of black dots at a relatively short distance from each other, about 1,000 km. They subsequently move away from each other and reach their maximum size. It is common for two of the group, located at roughly the same solar latitude, to grow larger than others. One of these precedes the others in the direction of the Sun's rotation about its axis. This is called the p-spot (preceding). That which follows is called the f-spot (following). An average size sunspot is about 10,000 km wide. It is not uncommon for sunspots to reach 80,000 to 100,000 km, when they become visible from Earth to the naked eye at sunset.

Sunspots only last a few days on average, although the very large ones may last longer, about 100 days or 4 solar rotations.

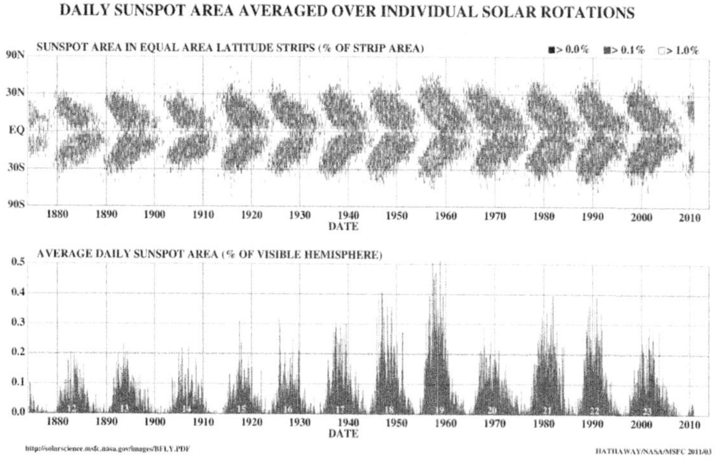

Figure 2.7-3. Butterfly diagram (Maunder diagram) (above). 11 year cycle of percentage surface coverage of the Sun by sunspots (below). (Source: NASA)

95% of sunspots last for less than 11 days. The number of sunspots and groups of sunspots follows an 11 year cycle of increase and decrease (Figure 2.7-3).

A sunspot's magnetic field displays the following specific characteristic: it extends outwards from its umbra towards the surface of the sun into a neighboring sunspot of opposite polarity. Thus, the polarity of the preceding sunspot is almost always different from that which follows. The polarity of preceding sunspots in the northern hemisphere is different from that in the southern hemisphere and displays a reversal approximately every 11 years. Essentially, the cycle of activity is 22 years, if we take into account the reversal of polarity.

The spots begin their cycle within a zone 40° north and south of the solar equator and as they reach the end of the 11 year period they converge towards this. Then they begin a new 11 year cycle with reverse polarity. The distribution of sunspots over the heliographic latitude is shown in the form of a butterfly or Maunder diagram (Figure 2.7-3).

The rotation of the Sun about its axis takes 27 days at the equator, and slows as the heliographic latitude increases. Sunspots close to the equator move 13.3° a day from east to west. Sunspots take 13.5 days to cross the visible side of the Sun on the equator.

The effect of sunspots on our Earth is huge, although we have yet to evaluate the extent of this. First of all, sunspots affect our climate. Secondly, they affect the growth of trees and plants. Maximum sunspot activity coincides with maximum growth in trees, usually during hot rainy periods. During Maunder's "Minimum" period, 1645-1715, it was observed that the complete absence of sunspots coincided with the Little Ice Age, during which rivers froze over and snows failed to thaw at lower altitudes.

2. Solar activity

Solar activity is essentially radiation from the Sun, which fluctuates over an 11 year period, following the sunspot cycle. Only during the last few decades have scientists been able, with the help of satellites, to measure the fluctuations in solar activity. Without satellites it was impossible to detect or study solar radiation. Whilst the fluctuations during the 11-year cycle range from 0.1 to 0.2%, the impact of these fluctuations on the climate, nature and human life, is highly significant.

The solar wind is composed of ionized particles, mainly protons and electrons, which are released at huge speeds and scattered throughout our Solar System. The Earth is protected against ionized protons and other particles in the solar wind, which can reach the Earth within 30 minutes, by its magnetosphere, a shield created by its magnetic field. One of the optical effects of solar wind is the Aurora Borealis. Sudden fluctuations in the solar wind can cause geomagnetic storms on Earth, with great implications for power distribution networks, telecommunications satellites and, to some extent, people.

Solar radiation is considered to have an impact at two main levels:

1. the upper atmosphere,
2. the lower atmosphere and the surface of the Earth.

3. Sunspots as an Astrological parameter

Another variable which may, however, be considered to affect the temperament of each person is the number of active sunspots at the time of their birth. This is a potentially important parameter; it is clear to all that the effect on a child's personality may be different if they are born at a time when the Earth is being bombarded by solar wind as opposed to a time in which solar activity is minimal.

According to research by the Japanese haematologist, Dr. Maki Tanaka, there is a link between changes in the albumin level of the blood and the level of solar activity and the number of sunspots. This phenomenon was named the "Tanaka Phenomenon" in his honor. Tanaka also constructed an index of measurement for the level of albumin in the blood (albumin is a protein produced in the liver. It is the protein with the highest concentration in the blood. A decrease in albumin and overall blood protein may be related to damage or functional impairment of the liver, as well as other diseases).

The Tanaka index increases during surges in solar activity, and declines during solar eclipses.

We consider that the intensity of the solar wind (and the number of sunspots) is directly related to a person's idiosyncrasies and temperament.

Of course, what precedes this are the hereditary characteristics which are indelibly written in a child's DNA.

Number of Sunspots	Temperament	Symbol
0 to 10	Mild natured	α
10 to 20	Relaxed and peaceful	β
20 to 30	Gentle, peace-loving	γ
30 to 40	Slightly driven, ambitious	δ
40 to 50	Animated, but seeks harmony	ε
50 to 60	Balanced emotions	ζ
60 to 70	Dynamic	η
70 to 80	Vivacious	θ
80 to 90	Irritable, prone to snap decisions	ι
90 to 100	Strong tempered	κ
100 to 110	Intense, untamed	λ
110 to 130	Quick to anger	μ
130 to 160	Hyperactive	ν
160 or more	Explosive	ξ

Table describing the relationship between the number of sunspots and temperament

From an astrological perspective, the number of sunspots can indicate a tendency towards certain temperamental characteristics; according to others, they may activate certain sections of the genetic code which may predetermine specific personal characteristics.

The table above can interpret many of the unexplained factors in Western Astrology. It can show how it is possible that a child born under a 'naturally balanced' sign can be irritable and wild, passionate and driven (due to a high number of sunspots). It may even explain why people expected to be impulsive and aggressive show completely opposite temperaments (due to the low number of sunspots).

Chapter 8

Construction of a Horoscope under the Thirteen Signs of the Zodiac

1. An example

Let us construct step by step a Natal Horoscope based on the Thirteen Zodiac Sign system. Our man (Dimitris) was born in Greece on 29/3/1980 at 13:00.

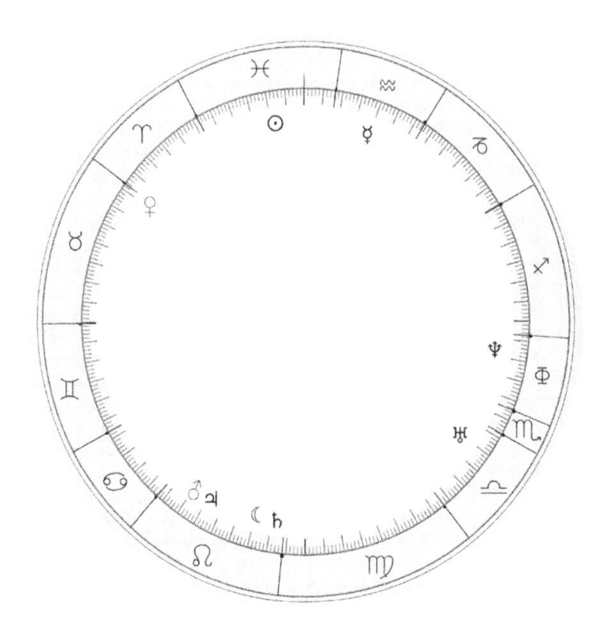

Figure 2.8-1

In the figure, we can see the actual zodiac circle starting from point "γ". Its beginning is at 12 o'clock, represented by the small vertical line on the uppermost part of the circle. Moving in an anticlockwise direction, the circle portrays the zodiac constellations in the order in which they appear in the sky: Pisces – Aries – Taurus – Gemini – Cancer – Leo – Virgo – Libra – Scorpio – Ophiuchus – Sagittarius – Capricorn – Aquarius.

First of all, our man is born in Pisces and not Aries as Western Astrology would have it. In other words, the Sun was in Pisces at the moment of his birth. The Moon was in Leo, so his Ascendant is Leo.

Based on his Sign of the Zodiac:
Dimitris is a dynamic character who likes to exercise control over his life. He faces adversity with courage and, whenever he finds himself in a difficult position, he will come up with new ideas to restore balance.

Based on his Ascendant:
The Moon in Leo indicates humility and modesty. He shows prudence and abides by the rules. He is conscientious and organizes his finances well.

Based on Sunspots:
When he was born, the Sun had 190 sunspots, a very large number indicating intense solar activity. Because of this, Dimitris displays an irritability and tension in his relationships, which Western Astrology would be hard put to explain.

Based on the Planetary Aspects:
Mercury and the Moon are in opposition, which is interpreted as a tendency towards emotional communication and success in sexual relationships. The opposition of Venus to Uranus in-

dicates strong friendships and good relationships with friends. The conjunction of Mars with Jupiter indicates conflict in the family environment. Lastly, the conjunction of the Moon with Saturn indicates impulsiveness with regard to material things and selfishness in sex.

If we compare this Horoscope, constructed according to the 13 Zodiac Sign system, with that of Chapter 3 in the first part of this book, we will see that they describe two very different people, but all scientific evidence clearly advocates the Horoscope suggested under the 13 Zodiac Sign system.

1. Step-by-Step Construction

Firstly, we draw a large circle using compasses, as in Figure 2.8-2. Next, we use a protractor to measure the angles and arcs on the circumference of our circle.

Starting from point "γ", which is in the (virtual) 12 o'clock position, we draw a line to the center of the circle and measure 8.2° to the right. This will take us to the boundary of Aquarius (which is where point "γ" will be in approximately 600 years).

From this point - let us call it Y - we measure 37° to the left in an anticlockwise direction. These 37 degrees represent Pisces. From the point representing the end of the Pisces section, let's say point I, we measure 24.8° for Aries – up to point K – then subsequently 36.7° for Taurus, 27.8° for Gemini, 20.1° for Cancer, 35.8° for Leo, 44° for Virgo, 23.2° for Libra, 6.6° for Scorpio, 18.6° for Ophiuchus, 33.4° for Sagittarius, 27.8° for Capricorn and, lastly, 24.2°for Aquarius, which will take us back to point Y.

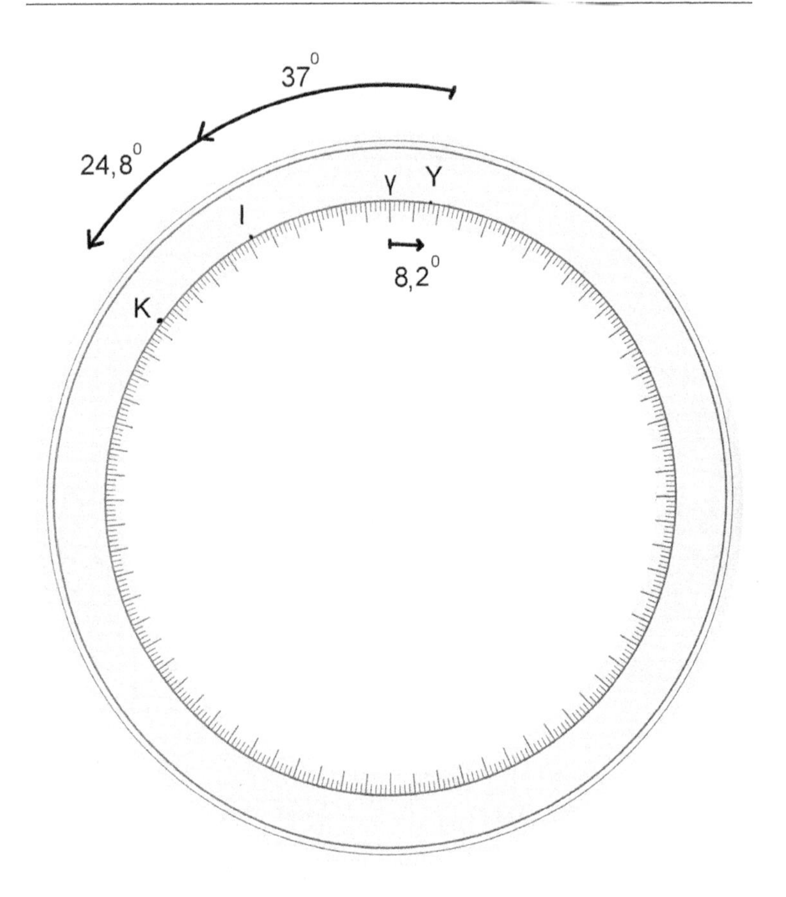

Figure 2.8-2: Construction of the new zodiac circle.
First move 8.2° to the right and then 37° to the left… etc.

Adding all the degrees of the zodiac together will give us 360°, i.e. a full circle. It should be clarified at this point that all the arc lengths described for each constellation of the zodiac arise from scientific data based on the constellation divisions made by the International Astronomical Union (IAU). Details can be found on the website http://www.astrology13.com. In Appendix I of the book, you will find a circle divided according to the exact positions of the zodiac constellations as they are in the sky, so that you can try completing your own natal horoscope.

The date of birth is known; we are only interested in the accuracy of the time to within one or two hours, unless the Moon happens to be on the borderline between two zodiac signs, in which case greater accuracy would be necessary.

The tables giving the positions of the planets, the Sun and the Moon on the Ecliptic are available from the Jet Propulsion Laboratory at NASA: http://ssd.jpl.nasa.gov/horizons.cgi#top .

Records are kept here of the positions of the planets, and much more besides. This site allows the free downloading of the actual positions of the planets, as well as variable No. 31, which gives the ecliptic coordinates of each celestial body. We are basically interested in the date and the ecliptic coordinate, and more specifically the ecliptic length which is measured from point "γ" to the left in degrees. For example, the position of the Sun on 29/03/1980 pursuant to the NASA data was 8.55° to the left of point γ. The position of Venus was 53.55° and that of Mercury 341.34° left of γ. (See Figure 2.8-1)

We are not finished yet, however, because we still need the key variable of the number of sunspots, although there is a small issue here because records of sunspots start from 1710. These records are available from the SIDC, the Solar Influences Data Analysis Center on the website

http://sidc.oma.be/LatestSWData/LatestSWData.php

In the left-hand column of the page, under "Sunspots → Data", we can find all the annual records of sunspots since 1818 as well as the smoothed monthly number of sunspots from 1749 onwards.

The zodiac circle of Western Astrology loses 50.2" (seconds of a degree) per year, or 1° each 72 years, due to the precession of the equinoxes. Under the 13 Zodiac Sign system, the zodiac circle is adjusted each year by 50.2" so that it is always updated to represent the exact positions of the zodiac constellations and the planets.

Chapter 9

The Characteristics of the Signs of the Zodiac

We will now present the characteristics and personality traits of each zodiac sign as they arise from astrological analysis under the 13 Zodiac Sign system. Undoubtedly, a description of a person's character also involves analysis of other factors, such as the Ascendant (that is, the position of the Moon), the positions of the planets and their aspects, as well as sunspots, as we saw in the previous chapter.

The dates on which the Sun enters the corresponding zodiac constellation in the year 2012 – 2013 are also included in the description. Those born on earlier dates – that is, all of us - must subtract (or in some cases, add) a certain amount of time. This depends, as we have emphasized, on precession, but also on a more complex motion, the Earth's "wobble" or nutation, which may change the boundaries of zodiac constellations by a few hours irrespective of the overall movement of 50.2" (seconds of a degree) per year.

Adjustment tables showing the boundaries of each zodiac constellation according to year of birth are presented in Appendix II. These are based on Greenwich Mean Time (GMT). Let us not be too quick to identify our zodiac sign before looking at the table which corresponds to our date of birth. Four examples are shown below for people born on 12 March at 1:30 Greek time. The corresponding GMT is 23:30 on 11th March (1:30 – 2.00 hours = 23: 30).

1. For a person aged 19 (in March 2012), based on the tables in Appendix II, the following applies: The Sun enters Pisces on 12th March 1993 at 3:20, and exits on 18th April 1993 at 15:20. Consequently, this person's Sign will be Aquarius, because on 11th March 1993, at 23:30, the Sun was still in Aquarius.
2. For a person aged 37 (in March 2012), based on the tables in Appendix II, the following applies: The Sun enters Pisces on 12th March 1975 at 12:30, and exits on 19th April 1975 at 00:30. Consequently, this person's Sign will be Aquarius, because on 11th March 1975, at 23:30, the Sun was still in Aquarius.
3. For a person aged 55 (in March 2012), based on the tables in Appendix II, the following applies: The Sun enters Pisces on 11th March 1957 at 21:40, and exits on 18th April 1957 at 10:00. Consequently, this person's Sign will be Pisces, because on 11th March 1957, at 23:30, the Sun was in Pisces.

4. For a person aged 73 (in March 2012), based on the tables in Appendix II, the following applies: The Sun enters Pisces on 11th March 1939 at 07:00, and exits on 18th April 1939 at 19:00. Consequently, this person's Sign will be Pisces, because on 11th March 1939, at 23:30, the Sun was in Pisces.

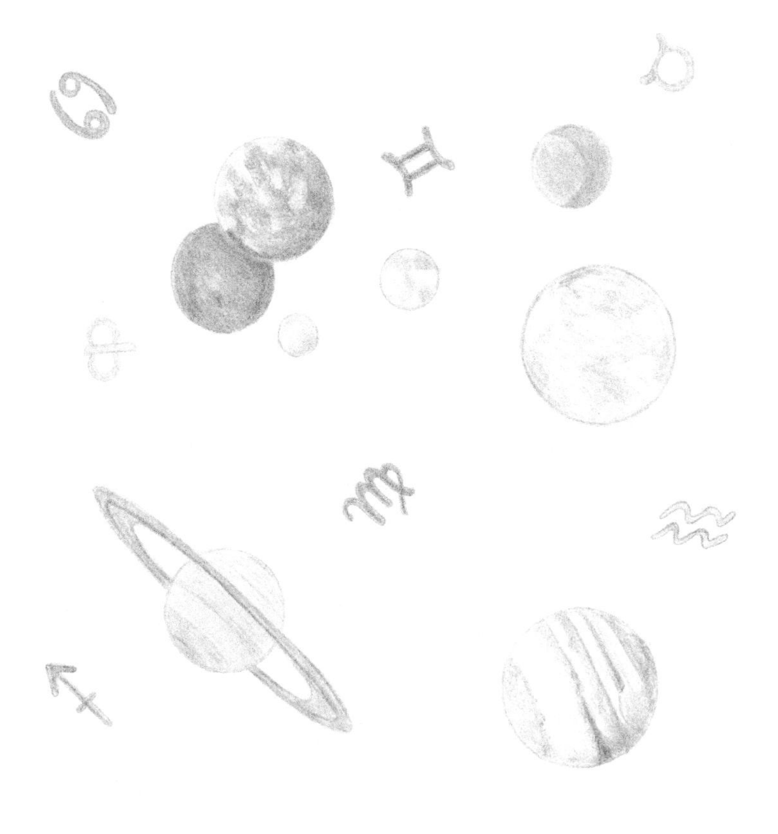

Figure 9-1: Planets and Zodiac symbols (by Maria Kanata)

♓

Pisces

Sun in Pisces from March 12, 00:20 to April 18, 2012, 12:20

Pisceans are now the leaders of the zodiac circle. They are the starting point. Thus, they are also leaders in life, with confidence in themselves. They are multifaceted and multitalented, and like to take the initiative under any circumstances. They are inspired by and represent springtime, the rebirth of nature, a new beginning. They have the strength and will-power to fight for their values and ideals. They can easily get carried away, but never give up in the face of difficulties. They freely express anything worrying them. They are impatient; they want it all, now!

Though they have the will to be in the driver's seat, they are not helped by their lack of discipline. They are hasty and often reckless, and can lose sight of their objectives due to their superficial approach to things. They are often quick-tempered due to their passionate and impulsive natures. They can be rebellious and stubborn, due to their self-centeredness.

Romantic Relationships & Love Life

In their love life, they tend to have intense passionate relationships and frequent arguments. Their leadership tendencies can impede their relationships with the opposite sex and their search for a balanced love life is a persistent problem.

Work & Career

At work, Pisceans are competitive and talented. They are capable of managing and guiding a company to success. Sometimes their talents are overshadowed by less competent colleagues, which will provoke simmering anger.

♈
Aries

Sun in Aries from April 18, 12:20 to May 13, 2012, 23:50

Arians epitomize stability. Their practical minds, in combination with their patience, inspire a sense of security in those around them. They show strong resilience in the face of the hardships of life, and hang onto their ideals in difficult moments.

Aries people do not take risks easily, and they like routine in everyday life. They are extremely patient, and show exceptional endurance under pressure.

Aries lost its leading position on the ecliptic hundreds of years ago. Aries people now have other virtues, such as artistic concerns and a gentle character.

The weaknesses of Arians include frequent expression of rage and a weakness for material things. They are also stubborn and stick to a routine. They are financially insecure and tend to procrastinate.

Romantic Relationships & Love Life

In their love life, Arians are attractive and have style. They also have an intense sexuality. Despite their stable nature, they are emotionally insecure.

Work & Career

At work, Arians are much sought after for their resilience in difficult situations and their stability. They are people to be trusted, and they know how to take advantage of this.

♉

Taurus

Sun in Taurus from May 13, 23:50 to June 21, 2012, 7:10

Taureans have an adaptable nature and are naturally diplomatic. They often express dualism, in the best sense, but are not two-faced. They are practical and look ahead to the future realistically, without any illusions. Taureans have their feet planted firmly on the ground, and make use of their acute powers of observation. They have a subtle sense of humor, and a balanced appreciation of those around them.

Taureans have the tendency to know a little about everything, and have difficulty focusing on just one thing.

Negative qualities of Taureans are their stubbornness, their slow pace and their inconsistency. They are talkative and sometimes express aggression. They tend not to know what they want, and change their minds easily.

Romantic Relationships & Love Life

They like to play romantic games. They aim for and seek harmonious love in relationships with the opposite sex. Though they are generally adaptable, they do not accept compromises in love.

Work & Career

At work, Taureans are resourceful and eloquent. They are communicative, and a career in the media would suit them.

♊

Gemini

Sun in Gemini from June 21, 7:10 to July 20, 2012, 12:00

Geminis are sensitive, loving and compassionate. They know how to manage difficult situations. They are naturally well-liked. They have ambitions which often manifest themselves late in life. Geminis are capable of nurturing sensitivity in their role as parents. They do the right thing when they trust their instincts. They prefer not to reveal their intentions.

Negative aspects of their character include insecurity and a tendency to be defensive. They are also moody, overprotective, and anxious. Lastly, Geminis easily transfer their affections.

Romantic Relationships & Love Life

As is their nature, they look for tenderness in their romantic relationships. They are sensitive and their moods change easily. They are often passive and can remain in problematic relationships for no good reason.

Work & Career

Geminis have aspirations and the potential to achieve them in their chosen career. They are good co-workers and, avoiding great conflict with their colleagues, maintain a balance.

Cancer

Sun in Cancer from July 20, 12:00 to August 10, 2012, 11:10

Cancerians are enthusiastic people. They have many virtues, such as pride (in the positive sense), generosity and kindness. They inspire and have a positive effect on those around them. Their main trait is the capacity to enjoy life. They have great confidence in their beliefs. They are ambitious and creative. Their strong personalities are a passport to the success of their ambitions. However, when things go wrong, they recognize this immediately, and nip their plans in the bud.

In addition, they have a tendency to be dramatic, selfish and controlling. They are also excessive in their expression of feelings towards the people immediately surrounding them. They are naïve and others take advantage of this.

Romantic Relationships & Love Life

They show an intense eroticism and creative imagination in their relationships with the opposite sex. They are looking for true love and, when the moment comes, they will sacrifice everything for it.

Work & Career

At work, Cancerians show stability and enthusiasm; this makes them much sought after in the job market. They are also ambitious and are desirous of moving up the organizational hierarchy.

♌
Leo

Sun in Leo from August 10, 11:10 to September 16, 2012, 12:20

Leos have an ability to analyze and psychologize. They are conscientious and fair. They are innately discreet and unassuming. Other qualities are their sense of humour and high intelligence. They have a weakness for cleanliness. Their abilities in life are multiple and varied; they involve themselves in many things and generally succeed at them. Lastly, they are genuine and scrupulous in their social relationships. They keep a part of the splendour of the old Sign of Leo, to the extent that they have 10 days in common with it, a rare occurrence in the rest of the Signs. In this respect, they are gradually losing the charisma associated with the old Sign in favor of other qualities such as genuineness and fairness.

In other respects, they are perfectionists and can often be submissive. They can often annoy their friends by being pompous or overenthusiastic.

Romantic Relationships & Love Life

They are capable of true love. They are discreet in their relationships, but they are looking for that one perfect love.

Work & Career

They are well-organized and meticulous at work, qualities which earn recognition and are rewarded by superiors. Additionally, their innate sense of justice makes the judiciary or legal profession an ideal career choice.

♍
Virgo

Sun in Virgo from September 16, 12:20 to October 31, 2012, 00:40

Virgos, above all, look for harmony in their lives. They are cooperative and seek peaceful relationships with those around them. They are highly perceptive and seek consensus. They know the importance of shared values and the sharing of material things. Another characteristic trait is the need for companionship and the recognition of friends. They like to work as part of a group and play a decisive role in shaping its perceptions. Virgos like to make others happy. They tend to cater to others' whims and gain immediate gratification from this. They also show good judgement, which often gets them out of difficult situations in life.

Their negative characteristics are narrow-mindedness, perfectionism and a tendency towards self-destruction. They sometimes undermine the goals of the wider social group to which they belong.

Romantic Relationships & Love Life

Virgos want to be charming and seductive. They are sexually motivated and look for harmony in their relationships. They are also very selective in their choice of romantic partners. They prefer to remain alone rather than start an uncertain relationship.

Work & Career

They are adaptable, and tend to be workaholics. They can be pivotal to work organization systems, in so far as these are based on good relations with colleagues. They have a natural inclination for diplomacy.

♎

Libra

Sun in Libra from October 31, 00:40 to November 23, 2012, 3:20

Librans are intuitive, visionary and perceptive. They show understanding of others, but are committed to their own goals. They may be the first to recognize a problem in a relationship, but will find it hard to externalize it. They are socially recognized. They participate in social affairs and will contribute their ideas to the whole. They have a great deal of pent up energy which, if they can bring themselves to use it positively, will allow them to progress far in life. Librans have extraordinary talents.

They are also suspicious of others, are very secretive, and like to be in control. They tend to have an existential anxiety, are often quiet, and can express intense jealousy.

Romantic Relationships & Love Life

They are characterized by their restless search for love. They often internalize their feelings. They look for sexual contact, but also for a genuine connection in their romantic relationships.

Work & Career

At work, they show a well-balanced and independent attitude. They are cooperative and conciliatory. They are perceptive, and people to be trusted in the workplace.

♏
Scorpio

Sun in Scorpio from November 23 3:20 to November 29, 2012, 15:30

Scorpios are extroverts and free thinkers. They are innately optimistic and enthusiastic. They especially like to have a good time with good friends. They are good-humoured and sociable. They also have a moral element, which plays a prominent role in their cultural orientation. They always hope for the best and are not easily put off by the difficult twists and turns of life. Happiness and good relationships are a way of life. They like to see the positive side of things; their philosophy of life is pragmatic and realistic.

The negative aspects of their character include a tendency towards excess and a disregard for social norms. They are restless and are attracted by adventure. They can sometimes be opportunistic.

Romantic Relationships & Love Life

In their romantic relationships they can be excessive. They instantly externalize their feelings, and seek an immediate response. They generally have intensely passionate relationships, with many ups and downs.

Work & Career

They are flexible and optimistic in the work domain. They are always well-prepared, and are appreciated by their superiors. They show commitment to their job, and work hard at career development.

Φ

Ophiuchus

Sun in Ophiuchus from November 29, 15:30 to December 17, 2012, 23:00

Those born under the sign of Ophiuchus tend to doubt everything. They have their own ideological approach and philosophy of life. They love to teach and are very effective teachers of the young. Among their characteristic traits are optimism and impulsiveness. They have an opinion about everything and will pursue their rights to express it to the end. They feel free and unfettered. Ophiuchus people are very active, with a positive energy which they channel into ambitious plans. Adventure is in their blood and they will seek it out in all its forms. They will use academic study to ground a well-organized attack on opposing ideologies.

In other respects, they may be curious, but can also be irresponsible. Their approach to things is often superficial. They have a tendency to excess in all aspects of their activities.

Romantic Relationships & Love Life

In romantic relationships Ophiuchus people are innocents. They are spontaneous with the opposite sex. They can also be frivolous in the expression of their feelings and may cause frustration. However, they can be adventurous lovers.

Work & Career

They have ambitions for their career, and if they choose the field of education, they show a talent for conveying knowledge. Generally, they are workaholics and people to be trusted in the workplace.

♐

Sagittarius

Sun in Sagittarius from December 17, 23:00, 2012 to January 19, 2013, 18:10

Sagittarians are responsible and favour discipline. They are characterized by a sense of duty towards society. They have a sense of humor, sometimes a little coarse, and they like to tease their friends. They have their own ideology, and love to put their philosophy into practice. Other characteristic traits are their organizing skills and their ability to bring people together in pursuit of a common goal. They are attracted by social acceptance. They are ambitious and work hard to preserve their status. They pay attention to detail and require strict observance of anything previously agreed. They are athletic and may devote themselves to achievement in the field of sports. They maintain the balance between people of opposing views and are often the sole point of contact between them.

Negative qualities include impulsiveness, conservatism and harshness, as well as narrow-mindedness, perfectionism and insecurity. Sometimes they appear overly serious, and their actions are generally deliberate.

Romantic Relationships & Love Life

Sagittarians are fickle in their romantic relationships. With maturity, they desire more permanent relationships. They immediately look for the one great love of their life.

Work & Career

The desire for power, their perfectionism and their tendency to be autocratic, characterize Sagittarians as employers in the workplace. As employees, they have considerable organizational skills and pay attention to detail. They have great potential for career development.

♑

Capricorn

Sun in Capricorn from January 19, 18:10 to February 16, 2013, 4:50

Capricorns are idealistic and altruistic. They are natural revolutionaries. They will be behind every reorganization and progressive development. They are attracted by science and research activities. They are always blatantly honest. They are characterized by their contemplative and persuasive nature. They wish to convince others only through discussion and dialectical reasoning. They are innately unpredictable and may suddenly back out of an agreement or negotiation. They can sometimes become avid supporters of outdated concepts.

Their negative qualities include eccentricity, a certain coldness in their dealings with those around them, and their intransigence. They are people of extremes, with an obvious desire to provoke.

Romantic Relationships & Love Life

They go to extremes in love, too. The passion in their romantic relationships is legendary. They look only for someone who is equally ideologically grounded, and are confrontational with them.

Work & Career

They are reflective and suited to intellectual occupations, provided that their family background equips them to exploit their talents. In all cases, they are devoted to their chosen careers. They take pride in setting difficult targets at work.

♒

Aquarius

Sun in Aquarius from February 16, 4:50 to March 12, 2013, 6:20

Aquarians have a rich imagination, which is an asset in their lives. They are compassionate and receptive, and cannot bear injustice. They are enraged by human exploitation. They are dreamers, and extremely sensitive. They are romantic and have a vision of society as it should be. They are idealists. They are intuitive, and put trust in their intuition. They adapt their lives on the basis of their experiences and know how to make compromises in their own best interests. To avoid hurting others, which they find emotionally oppressive, they do not find it easy to say no. Aquarians usually try to put themselves in the other person's shoes, so as to understand exactly what they are feeling.

Their negative qualities include indecisiveness in the face of critical decisions, a laid-back approach to things, impractical mysticism and self-delusion, and excessive fantasizing.

Romantic Relationships & Love Life

They have an intense desire for romance. They idealize their relationships and often pay the price. Their emotional attachments can break their hearts.

Work & Career

At work, Aquarians are inventive and resourceful. Because of this, they are much sought after. Their sensitivity can often make them victims of competitiveness in the workplace.

Chapter 10

A First Critique in Response to Western Astrologers

After January 2011, when the issue of the 13th Sign of the Zodiac was ignited by astronomer Parke Kunkle, Western Astrologers reacted with articles and interviews in the press and on the internet.

So what did they have to say about it all? They had three basic arguments, which are presented here together with our responses:

1. Western Astrologers say that modern Western Astrology is based on the seasons, and not on the constellations of the Zodiac and the stars. The seasons are measured by the Earth's orbit around the Sun and its passing through intersections of the celestial equator on the ecliptic, the so-called equinoxes.

Response: But modern Western Astrology is based on the tradition of the ancient Mesopotamian, Egyptian and primarily Hellenistic Astronomers, whose principles they adopted (mainly those of Claudius Ptolemy). Unfortunately for Western Astrologers, no theoretical foundation has appeared to date which supports the connection between Western Astrology and the seasons. They were always bound to the constellations of the Zodiac. Furthermore, the passage of the Sun through the points of the equinoxes has shifted by approximately 29.2°, leaving Western Astrology without any arguments to support this.

2. Western Astrologers now claim that the 12 Signs of the Zodiac do not correspond to the Zodiac constellations, except in name. So called Tropical (Western) Astrology is not based on the constellations, but rather on the conceptual significance of the 12 Signs, and therefore Astronomers are mistaken in attacking them in this respect.

Response: Making a virtue of necessity, tropical Astrologers now separate the concepts from the objects they derive from. Well, that is certainly one way to deal with it! Having no other cards to play, since reality continues to contradict them daily, they prefer to disengage the signs of the zodiac from their stars! ! Well, then why not separate the concept of the planets from the planets themselves? Or by extension why not separate the concept of a human being from human beings themselves, or the concept of an elephant from the elephant itself? Enough is enough! If Astrologers wish to adapt themselves to contemporary circumstances, there is a way: the Astrology of the 13 Signs of the Zodiac.

3. Western Astrologers say that the Tropical Zodiac is related to our existence, and that the Sidereal (or Vedic) Zodiac is related to cosmic questions.

Response: This so-called solution, which separates the two Zodiacs, leads to an astrological impasse. The Sidereal Zodiac, which ostensibly follows the precession of the equinoxes, rejects Ophiuchus, and therefore its adaptation to the boundaries of the Zodiac constellations is also inaccurate. Thus, both the Tropical Zodiac of Western Astrology and the Sidereal Zodiac of Vedic Astrology are deficient in their own ways.

Chapter 11

Walter Berg's Thirteen Signs of the Zodiac

The notion of adapting modern Astrology to the concept of the 13 Signs of the Zodiac began some years ago. In 1995, the British physicist Barry Parkinson published a book, under the pseudonym Walter Berg, entitled: "The 13 Signs of the Zodiac", and was the first to adopt what a realistic and scientific approach suggests – adaptation to include 13 Signs of the Zodiac.

The Astrology of Walter Berg lays the proper foundations for resolving the problem facing Astrology, but fails to overcome the outdated assumptions of Claudius Ptolemy. He accepts the four elements of the ancient world: earth, air, fire and water. He accepts the concept of male and female zodiac signs, as well the concept of ruling planets, once adapted to take into account their new positions. Lastly, he does not make it plain whether he accepts the Ascendant or the Midheaven in the form determined by Western Astrology, or all of its other outdated elements. In his book, he does not use the Ascendant (ASC), Midheaven (MC), Descendant (DESC) or the Nadir (IC). All of this weakens his theory. A planet cannot be considered to have its home in or to govern a particular zodiac constellation. The modern theory regarding the creation of our planetary system does not accept that the planets were created at a particular point on their orbit. Therefore no ruling planet can be assigned to any specific zodiac sign.

Fire cannot define a zodiac sign! The Ascendant cannot be left out of Astrology. We are not in the year 100 A.D.; this is the year 2012.

The symbol proposed by Walter Berg to represent Ophiuchus is the following:

Without doubt this symbol has little to do with Ophiuchus; it is simply the letter “U” with a horizontal wavy line, which could conceivably represent the snake.

We would like to propose a symbol for the zodiac sign of Ophiuchus, one which unequivocally represents it: the Greek letter Phi (Φ). This arises directly from the word OPHIUCHUS itself, and is most clearly characteristic of it.

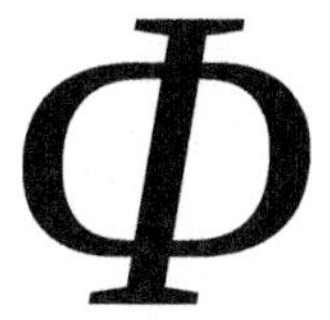

With the letter "Φ", we also have the synthesis of the first letter of the word Ophiuchus "O" with the letter "I" as the snake intersecting it vertically to give the ideal symbol.

To continue, we can see that Walter Berg's book merely presents the characteristics of the "New Signs of the Zodiac". For each sign of the zodiac, he analyzes personality, love life and relationships, career, health and the future, and, as we have already mentioned, he refers to the planetary houses of each sign of the zodiac, and whether they are fire, air, earth or water signs. Lastly, for each sign of the zodiac he indicates whether they are fixed, tropical, bicorporeal or equinoctial in accordance with Claudius Ptolemy's theory. He takes into account the positive and negative nature of the signs of the zodiac. He essentially develops a zodiac Astrology based on the position of the Sun. This tends to create more problems than it solves.

Refusing to come to grips with the Ascendant weakens his position and makes him easy prey for the claws of Western Astrology. It is not by chance that this model never prevailed. A fully-documented scientific foundation for the New Astrology is lacking, as is a comprehensive examination of all the aspects of the Old Astrology. In addition to the Ascendant, the aspects of the planets are also omitted. Berg writes something new without critiquing the old, or explaining why the new system should be used. In the introduction to his book, he essentially writes that if, all these years, astrological predictions have failed to correspond to your life, this is because the Zodiac constellations have changed, but under the New Signs of the Zodiac it will all fall into place. But is this enough?

In conclusion, it has to be said that Astrology as a whole must be brought up to date. All those elements holding it back in the past should be discarded, and only those based on scientific analysis should be retained.

Only the Astrology of the 13 Signs of the Zodiac as described in this book dares to look beyond the quaint notions of the past. It attempts to marry only those elements of the past which can be supported by science today. It proposes new variables, such as sunspots, and puts the Moon back on her pedestal. The Moon is the new Ascendant and rules the Astrology of the 21st century at the side of the Sun. The remaining planets have a secondary role, whilst planetary aspects in relation to the points of the horizon (i.e. the old Ascendants) are without meaning.

Epilogue

I am certain that there are two categories of people who will wish to respond to this book:

- Fellow physicists in order to demolish my arguments
- Astrologers in order to defend their flimsy constructs.

For physicists, of course, there are other much more pressing issues to be researched, such as the theory of everything, the search for new planets capable of sustaining life using the Kepler telescope, and the conducting of new experiments with the Hadron Collider at CERN.

However, above all these concerns is the need to find a new theory of the universe. In the year 2011, the worldwide community of physicists cannot possibly continue to rely on the prevailing theory of the Big Bang, invented by a priest, George Lemaître, for purely theological reasons.

They cannot continue to invoke new physical phenomena such as dark matter and dark energy in support of Father Lemaître's flawed model. It does not seem reasonable to theorize that visible matter accounts for only 4.6% of the whole and that the remainder is dark matter and energy!

We do not yet have sufficient evidence to reject the Big Bang theory, though the whole story reminds me of the theory of Claudius Ptolemy with regard to epicycles, before the coming of Kepler and Newton.

Astrologers have a new golden opportunity to adapt to the new circumstances. If Ptolemy were alive today and read that people were making astrological predictions using his model based on the position of point γ on the ecliptic in the year 83 A.D., he would be astounded.

Even Vedic Astrology, which approximately follows the actual positions of the constellations in the sky, is flawed. We can be much more precise today, yet it fails to determine either the actual boundaries of the zodiac constellations or to take the position of Ophiuchus into account. A person born with the Sun in Ophiuchus cannot be considered to be anything other than an OPHIUCHIAN.

Vasilis Kanatas

Bibliography

Ancient Writings

Aratus of Soli: *Phaenomena and Diosemeia* from the book *The Phaenomena and Diosemeia of Aratus of Soli*, Evaggelos Spandagos,
Pub. Aithra (Greek edition (Gr.))

Aristotle: *Physics*,
Pub. Cactus (Gr.)

Aristotle: *Metaphysics*,
Pub. Cactus (Gr.)

Achilles Tatios: *Regarding Everything*, Evaggelos Spandagos,
Pub. Aithra (Gr.)

Eratosthenes of Kyrenia: *On the Phaenomena of Aratus*, Evaggelos Spandagos,
Pub. Aithra (Gr.)

Eratosthenes of Kyrenia: Catasterismoi, *Placings among the Stars*, from the book *The Catasterismoi of Eratosthenes of Kyrenia*, Evaggelos Spandagos,
Pub. Aithra (Gr.)

Heraclitus: *On Nature*, Evaggelos Roussos,
Pub. Dim. N. Papadimas (Gr.)

Thales, Anaximander, Anaximenes,
Pub. Exantas, Trans. Dimitris Roussos (Gr.)

Claudius Ptolemy: *The Syron Apotelesmatica* or *Tetrabiblos*,
Pub. Cactus (Gr.)

Proclus: *Comments on the Tetrabiblos of Ptolemy*,
Pub. Cactus (Gr.)

Proclus: *Restatements of Ptolemy's Tetrabiblos*,
Pub. Odysseas Hatzopoulos (Gr.)

Hypsicles: *On Ascensions*, Evaggelos Spandagos,
Pub. Aithra (Gr.)

Astronomy - Uranography

Antonakopoulos, G. A.: *General Astronomy*,
Pub. Teaching Book Publication Organization (OEDB) 1986 (Gr.)

Zafeiropoulos, Vasilis: *Radio Astronomy*
Pub. University of Patras (Gr.)

Theodosios, Stratos,- Danezis, Manos: *The Stars and their Myths*
Pub. Diavlos 1991 (Gr.)

Kanatas, Vasilis: *On Constellations*, dissertation 1991. (Gr.)

Kostakis, D - Kontopoulos G.: Cosmology,
Pub. Spinger Verlag

Flammarion, Kamilos: *Popular Astronomy*,
Pub. Dimitrakos D. 1937 (Gr.)

Abbel, George: *Exploration of the Universe*

Hawking, S.: *A Brief History of Time*,
Pub. Katoptro

Heng, Kevin: *The Mathematics of Astrology: does House Division Make Sense?*

Kaler, James: *Stars and their Spectra*,
Pub. Cambridge University Press, 1989

Karkoschka, E.: *The Observer's Sky Atlas*,
Pub. Springer Verlag 1988

Martens, Ronny and Trachet, Tim: *Making Sense of Astrology*
Pub. Prometheus Books, 1998

Sanford, John: *Observing the Constellations*,
Pub. Simon & Schuster Inc.

Weinberg, Steven: *The First Three Minutes*,
Pub. Eirmos 1991

Astrology – History – Philosophy

Kassa, Olga: *Astrology, the Art of Casting Horoscopes,* Pub. Iamblikos 2002 (Gr.)
Kerenev: *Greek Mythology*, Pub. Kollarou Estias (Gr.)
Laou, T.: *Chinese Astrology*, Pub. Cactus (Gr.)
Bitsaki, Evtichi: *Nature in Dialectic Philosophy,* Pub. Synchroni Epochi (Gr.)
Spandagos, Evaggelos - Spandagou, Roula: *The Astronomers of Ancient Greece*, Pub. Aithra (Gr.)
Abbamonte, Mary Francis: *The 13th Sign,* Pub. 1st Books Library, 2002
Allen, Richard Hinckley: *Star Names, Their Lore and Meaning,* Pub. Dover
Beck, Roger: *A brief history of Ancient Astrology* Pub. Blackwell
Berg, Walter: *The Thirteen Signs of the Zodiac: Discover Who You Really Are with the New Sun Signs* Pub. Thorsons
Bonatus, Guido: *Anima Astrologia*
Gauquelin, Michel: *Astrology and Science,* Pub. Peter Davis
Gauquelin, Michel: *Cosmic Influences on Human Behavior: The Planetary Factors in Personality*
Hall, Judy: The Astrology Bible, Pub. Isorropon (Gr.)
Kasak, Enn: *Ancient Astrology as a common root for Science and Pseudo-Science,*
Web article: http://haldjas.folklore.ee/folklore
Lilly, William: *Christian Astrology*
Marshall, Peter: *World Astrology,* Pub. Oceanida 2007 (Gr.)

Miller I. Arthur: *Jung – Pauli: the Psychoanalyst, the Physicist and the Number 137* Travlos 2010 (Gr.)
Parker, Julia & Derek: *Astrology* Pub. Ellinika Grammata (Gr.)
Parker, Julia & Derek: *Astrology, Science and the Secrets of Studying the Stars* Pub. DK, ΣΚΑΪ
Schmidt, Robert: *Hellenistic Astrology: an Overview,* (Article from Project Hindsight)
Seymour, Percy: *Astrology: The Evidence of Science*
Seymour, Percy: *The Scientific Basis of Astrology: Tuning to the Music of the Planets* Pub. Quantum 1997
St. Clair, Marisa: *Sun & Moon Signs,* Pub. Grange Books 2008

APPENDIX I

Zodiac Circle 2012

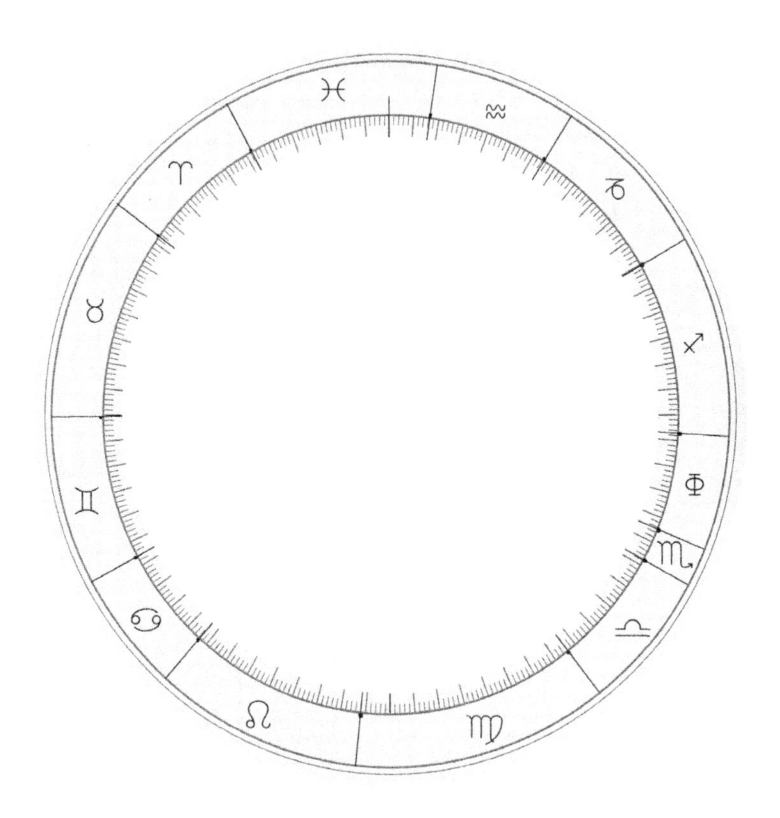

APPENDIX II

TABLES SHOWING THE DATES FOR THE 13 CONSTELLATIONS OF THE ZODIAC

The dates are based on Greenwich Mean Time. To find the time in other countries, it is necessary to convert it to GMT and then look at the respective table - the table for the year which is closest to your date of birth.

For each sign of the Zodiac you can see the date and time the Sun enters the constellation. The exit of the Sun from the boundaries of the constellation is shown directly below, that is, on the day and at the time the Sun moves into the next constellation.

	1930-31	1931-32	1932-33	1933-34	1934-35	1935-36
PSC ♓	11/3, 23:40	12/3, 5:40	11/3, 11:50	11/3, 18:00	12/3, 00:10	12/3, 6:20
ARI ♈	18/4, 12:00	18/4, 17:50	18/4, 00:00	18/4, 6:20	18/4, 12:20	18/4, 18:30
TAU ♉	13/5, 23:30	14/5, 5:30	13/5, 11:40	13/5, 17:50	14/5, 00:00	14/5, 6:00
GEM ♊	21/6, 7:00	21/6, 13:00	20/6, 19:20	21/6, 1:30	21/6, 7:30	21/6, 13:40
CNC ♋	20/7, 11:40	20/7, 17:50	20/7, 00:10	20/7, 6:20	20/7, 12:20	20/7, 18:30
LEO ♌	10/8, 10:40	10/8, 16:50	9/8, 23:00	10/8, 5:20	10/8, 11:20	10/8, 17:30
VIR ♍	16/9, 11:50	16/9, 18:00	16/9, 00:20	16/9, 6:30	16/9, 12:30	16/9, 18:50
LIB ♎	31/10, 00:00	31/10, 6:20	30/10, 12:20	30/10, 18:30	31/10, 00:40	31/10, 6:50
SCO ♏	23/11, 1:40	23/11, 7:50	22/11, 14:00	22/11, 20:10	23/11, 2:20	23/11, 8:30
OPH ⛎	29/11, 14:50	29/11, 21:10	29/11, 3:10	29/11, 9:20	29/11, 15:30	29/11, 21:40
SGR ♐	17/12, 22:20	18/12, 4:30	17/12, 10:40	17/12, 16:40	17/12, 22:50	18/12, 5:00
CAP ♑	19/1, 17:30	19/1, 23:40	19/1, 5:50	19/1, 11:50	19/1, 18:10	20/1, 00:10
AQR ♒	16/2, 4:00	16/2, 10:10	15/2, 16:20	15/2, 22:30	16/2, 4:40	16/2, 10:40
PSC ♓	12/3, 5:40	11/3, 11:50	11/3, 18:00	12/3, 00:10	12/3, 6:20	11/3, 12:20

	1936-37	1937-38	1938-39	1939-40	1940-41	1941-42
PSC ♓	11/3, 12:20	11/3, 18:30	12/3, 00:40	12/3, 7:00	11/3, 13:10	11/3, 19:20
ARI ♈	18/4, 00:40	18/4, 6:40	18/4, 13:00	18/4, 19:00	18/4, 1:10	18/4, 7:30
TAU ♉	13/5, 12:10	13/5, 18:20	14/5, 00:30	14/5, 6:30	13/5, 12:40	13/5, 19:00
GEM ♊	20/6, 19:50	21/6, 2:00	21/6, 8:10	21/6, 14:00	20/6, 20:20	21/6, 2:40
CNC ♋	20/7, 00:40	20/7, 6:40	20/7, 13:00	20/7, 19:00	20/7, 1:10	20/7, 7:20
LEO ♌	9/8, 23:50	10/8, 5:50	10/8, 12:00	10/8, 18:10	10/8, 00:10	10/8, 6:30
VIR ♍	16/9, 1:00	16/9, 7:00	16/9, 13:10	16/9, 19:20	16/9, 1:30	16/9, 7:40
LIB ♎	30/10, 13:10	30/10, 19:10	31/10, 1:20	30/10, 7:30	30/10, 13:40	30/10, 19:50
SCO ♏	22/11, 14:40	22/11, 20:50	23/11, 3:00	23/11, 9:20	22/11, 15:20	22/11, 21:30
OPH Φ	29/11, 3:50	29/11, 10:00	29/11, 16:10	29/11, 22:20	29/11, 4:30	29/11, 10:40
SGR ♐	17/12, 11:10	17/12, 17:20	17/12, 23:40	18/12, 5:50	17/12, 11:50	17/12, 18:00
CAP ♑	19/1, 6:20	19/1, 12:40	19/1, 18:50	20/1, 1:00	19/1, 7:10	19/1, 13:10
AQR ♒	15/2, 16:50	15/2, 23:10	16/2, 5:20	16/2, 11:30	15/2, 17:40	15/2, 23:50
PSC ♓	11/3, 18:30	12/3, 00:40	12/3, 7:00	11/3, 13:10	11/3, 19:20	12/3, 1:30

	1942-43	1943-44	1944-45	1945-46	1946-47	1947-48
PSC ♓	12/3, 1:30	12/3, 7:40	11/3, 13:40	11/3, 19:50	12/3, 2:00	12/3, 8:10
ARI ♈	18/4, 13:40	18/4, 19:50	18/4, 1:50	18/4, 8:00	18/4, 14:20	18/4, 20:20
TAU ♉	14/5, 1:10	14/5, 7:20	13/5, 13:30	13/5, 19:40	14/5, 1:50	14/5, 7:50
GEM ♊	21/6, 8:40	21/6, 14:50	20/6, 21:00	21/6, 3:10	21/6, 9:20	21/6, 15:20
CNC ♋	20/7, 13:20	20/7, 19:40	20/7, 1:50	20/7, 8:00	20/7, 14:10	20/7, 20:10
LEO ♌	10/8, 12:30	10/8, 18:40	10/8, 1:00	10/8, 7:00	10/8, 13:10	10/8, 19:20
VIR ♍	16/9, 13:40	16/9, 19:50	16/9, 2:00	16/9, 8:10	16/9, 14:20	16/9, 20:30
LIB ♎	31/10, 2:00	31/10, 8:00	30/10, 14:10	30/10, 20:20	31/10, 2:30	31/10, 8:50
SCO ♏	23/11, 3:40	23/11, 9:50	22/11, 16:00	22/11, 22:10	23/11, 4:20	23/11, 10:30
OPH Φ	29/11, 16:50	29/11, 22:50	29/11, 5:00	29/11, 11:10	29/11, 17:20	29/11, 23:30
SGR ♐	18/12, 00:10	18/12, 6:20	17/12, 12:30	17/12, 18:30	18/12, 00:50	18/12, 6:50
CAP ♑	19/1, 19:30	20/1, 1:30	19/1, 7:40	19/1, 13:50	19/1, 20:00	20/1, 2:00
AQR ♒	16/2, 6:00	16/2, 12:10	15/2, 18:10	16/2, 00:20	16/2, 6:30	16/2, 12:40
PSC ♓	12/3, 7:40	11/3, 13:40	11/3, 19:50	12/3, 2:00	12/3, 8:10	12/3, 14:10

	1948-49	1949-50	1950-51	1951-52	1952-53	1953-54
PSC ♓	11/3, 14:10	11/3, 20:20	12/3, 2:40	12/3, 8:50	11/3, 15:00	11/3, 21:10
ARI ♈	18/4, 2:20	18/4, 8:40	18/4, 14:50	18/4, 21:00	18/4, 3:10	18/4, 9:20
TAU ♉	13/5, 14:00	13/5, 20:10	14/5, 2:20	14/5, 8:20	13/5, 14:40	13/5, 20:50
GEM ♊	20/6, 21:40	21/6, 3:50	21/6, 9:50	21/6, 16:00	20/6, 22:10	21/6, 4:20
CNC ♋	20/7, 2:30	20/7, 8:40	20/7, 14:40	20/7, 20:50	20/7, 3:00	20/7, 9:10
LEO ♌	10/8, 1:30	10/8, 7:40	10/8, 13:40	10/8, 19:50	10/8, 2:10	10/8, 8:10
VIR ♍	16/9, 2:40	16/9, 9:00	16/9, 14:50	16/9, 21:10	16/9, 3:20	16/9, 9:20
LIB ♎	30/10, 14:50	30/10, 21:00	31/10, 3:10	31/10, 9:20	30/10, 15:30	30/10, 21:40
SCO ♏	22/11, 16:50	22/11, 22:50	23/11, 5:00	23/11, 11:20	22/11, 17:20	22/11, 23:30
OPH Φ	29/11, 5:40	29/11, 11:50	29/11, 18:00	30/11, 00:10	29/11, 6:20	29/11, 12:30
SGR ♐	17/12, 13:00	17/12, 19:20	18/12, 1:30	18/12, 7:40	17/12, 13:50	17/12, 19:50
CAP ♑	19/1, 8:10	19/1, 14:30	19/1, 20:40	20/1, 2:50	19/1, 9:00	19/1, 15:10
AQR ♒	15/2, 18:50	16/2, 1:00	16/2, 7:10	16/2, 13:20	15/2, 19:30	16/2, 1:40
PSC ♓	11/3, 20:20	12/3, 2:40	12/3, 8:50	11/3, 15:00	11/3, 21:10	12/3, 3:20

	1954-55	1955-56	1956-57	1957-58	1958-59	1959-60
PSC ♓	12/3, 3:20	12/3, 9:30	11/3, 15:30	11/3, 21:40	12/3, 4:00	12/3, 10:00
ARI ♈	18/4, 15:30	18/4, 21:30	18/4, 3:40	18/4, 10:00	18/4, 16:00	18/4, 22:10
TAU ♉	14/5, 3:00	14/5, 9:10	13/5, 15:10	13/5, 21:30	14/5, 3:30	14/5, 9:40
GEM ♊	21/6, 10:40	21/6, 16:40	20/6, 22:50	21/6, 5:10	21/6, 11:00	21/6, 17:10
CNC ♋	20/7, 15:20	20/7, 21:30	20/7, 3:40	20/7, 9:50	20/7, 15:50	20/7, 22:00
LEO ♌	10/8, 14:20	10/8, 20:30	10/8, 2:40	10/8, 9:00	10/8, 15:00	10/8, 21:00
VIR ♍	16/9, 15:30	16/9, 21:40	16/9, 3:50	16/9, 10:10	16/9, 16:10	16/9, 22:20
LIB ♎	31/10, 3:40	31/10, 10:00	30/10, 16:00	30/10, 22:10	31/10, 4:20	31/10, 10:30
SCO ♏	23/11, 5:40	23/11, 11:50	22/11, 18:00	23/11, 00:10	23/11, 6:20	23/11, 12:30
OPH Φ	29/11, 18:40	30/11, 00:50	29/11, 6:50	29/11, 13:00	29/11, 19:10	30/11, 1:20
SGR ♐	18/12, 2:10	18/12, 8:10	17/12, 14:20	17/12, 20:20	18/12, 2:30	18/12, 8:50
CAP ♑	19/1, 21:20	20/1, 3:20	19/1, 9:30	19/1, 15:40	19/1, 21:50	20/1, 4:00
AQR ♒	16/2, 7:50	16/2, 14:00	15/2, 20:10	16/2, 2:20	16/2, 8:20	16/2, 14:30
PSC ♓	12/3, 9:30	11/3, 15:30	11/3, 21:40	12/3, 4:00	12/3, 10:00	11/3, 16:10

	1960-61	1961-62	1962-63	1963-64	1964-65	1965-66
PSC ♓	11/3, 16:10	11/3, 22:20	12/3, 4:30	12/3, 10:40	11/3, 16:50	11/3, 23:00
ARI ♈	18/4, 4:20	18/4, 10:20	18/4, 16:40	18/4, 22:40	18/4, 4:50	18/4, 11:10
TAU ♉	13/5, 15:50	13/5, 22:00	14/5, 4:10	14/5, 10:10	13/5, 16:20	13/5, 22:40
GEM ♊	20/6, 23:20	21/6, 5:30	21/6, 11:40	21/6, 17:40	21/6, 00:00	21/6, 6:20
CNC ♋	20/7, 4:10	20/7, 10:20	20/7, 16:30	20/7, 22:30	20/7, 4:50	20/7, 11:00
LEO ♌	10/8, 3:20	10/8, 9:20	10/8, 15:30	10/8, 21:40	10/8, 3:50	10/8, 10:00
VIR ♍	16/9, 4:30	16/9, 10:30	16/9, 16:40	16/9, 22:50	16/9, 5:00	16/9, 11:20
LIB ♎	30/10, 16:40	30/10, 22:50	31/10, 5:00	31/10, 11:10	30/10, 17:20	30/10, 23:30
SCO ♏	22/11, 18:40	23/11, 00:50	23/11, 7:10	23/11, 13:10	22/11, 19:20	23/11, 1:30
OPH Φ	29/11, 7:30	29/11, 13:40	29/11, 19:50	30/11, 2:00	29/11, 8:10	29/11, 14:20
SGR ♐	17/12, 15:00	17/12, 21:10	18/12, 3:20	18/12, 9:30	17/12, 15:30	17/12, 21:50
CAP ♑	19/1, 10:10	19/1, 16:20	19/1, 22:40	20/1, 4:40	19/1, 10:50	19/1, 17:00
AQR ♒	15/2, 20:40	16/2, 2:50	16/2, 9:10	16/2, 15:10	15/2, 21:20	16/2, 3:40
PSC ♓	11/3, 22:20	12/3, 4:30	12/3, 10:40	11/3, 16:50	11/3, 23:00	12/3, 5:10

	1966-67	1967-68	1968-69	1969-70	1970-71	1971-72
PSC ♓	12/3, 5:10	12/3, 11:20	11/3, 17:20	11/3, 23:40	12/3, 5:40	12/3, 11:50
ARI ♈	18/4, 17:10	18/4, 23:30	18/4, 5:30	18/4, 11:30	18/4, 17:50	19/4, 00:00
TAU ♉	14/5, 4:40	14/5, 11:00	13/5, 17:10	13/5, 23:10	14/5, 5:20	14/5, 11:30
GEM ♊	21/6, 12:20	21/6, 18:30	21/6, 00:40	21/6, 6:40	21/6, 13:00	21/6, 19:00
CNC ♋	20/7, 16:50	20/7, 23:20	20/7, 5:30	20/7, 11:40	20/7, 17:50	20/7, 23:50
LEO ♌	10/8, 16:00	10/8, 22:20	10/8, 4:40	10/8, 10:40	10/8, 16:50	10/8, 23:00
VIR ♍	16/9, 17:20	16/9, 23:30	16/9, 5:50	16/9, 11:50	16/9, 18:00	17/9, 00:10
LIB ♎	31/10, 5:30	31/10, 11:40	30/10, 17:50	31/10, 00:00	31/10, 6:10	31/10, 12:20
SCO ♏	23/11, 7:30	23/11, 14:00	22/11, 20:00	23/11, 2:00	23/11, 8:20	23/11, 14:30
OPH Φ	29/11, 20:20	30/11, 2:40	29/11, 8:40	29/11, 14:40	29/11, 21:00	30/11, 3:20
SGR ♐	18/12, 3:40	18/12, 10:00	17/12, 16:10	17/12, 22:10	18/12, 4:30	18/12, 10:40
CAP ♑	19/1, 23:00	20/1, 5:20	19/1, 11:20	19/1, 17:20	19/1, 23:40	20/1, 5:50
AQR ♒	16/2, 9:40	16/2, 15:50	15/2, 22:00	16/2, 4:00	16/2, 10:10	16/2, 16:20
PSC ♓	12/3, 11:20	11/3, 17:20	11/3, 23:40	12/3, 5:40	12/3, 11:50	11/3, 18:00

	1972-73	1973-74	1974-75	1975-76	1976-77	1977-78
PSC ♓	11/3, 18:00	12/3, 00:00	12/3, 6:20	12/3, 12:30	11/3, 18:40	12/3, 1:00
ARI ♈	18/4, 5:50	18/4, 12:20	18/4, 18:30	19/4, 00:30	18/4, 6:50	18/4, 13:00
TAU ♉	13/5, 17:30	13/5, 23:50	14/5, 6:00	14/5, 12:00	13/5, 18:10	14/5, 00:30
GEM ♊	21/6, 1:00	21/6, 7:20	21/6, 13:20	21/6, 19:30	21/6, 1:50	21/6, 8:00
CNC ♋	20/7, 6:00	20/7, 12:10	20/7, 18:10	21/7, 00:20	20/7, 6:40	20/7, 12:40
LEO ♌	10/8, 5:00	10/8, 11:10	10/8, 17:20	10/8, 23:20	10/8, 5:40	10/8, 11:50
VIR ♍	16/9, 6:10	16/9, 12:30	16/9, 18:30	17/9, 00:40	16/9, 7:00	16/9, 12:50
LIB ♎	30/10, 18:30	31/10, 00:40	31/10, 6:50	31/10, 13:00	30/10, 19:10	31/10, 1:10
SCO ♏	22/11, 20:40	23/11, 3:00	23/11, 9:10	23/11, 15:00	22/11, 21:20	23/11, 3:30
OPH Φ	29/11, 9:20	29/11, 15:30	29/11, 21:40	30/11, 3:50	29/11, 10:00	29/11, 16:10
SGR ♐	17/12, 16:50	17/12, 23:10	18/12, 5:10	18/12, 11:20	17/12, 17:30	17/12, 23:30
CAP ♑	19/1, 11:50	19/1, 18:20	20/1, 00:30	20/1, 6:30	19/1, 12:40	19/1, 18:50
AQR ♒	15/2, 22:30	16/2, 4:50	16/2, 11:00	16/2, 17:00	15/2, 23:20	16/2, 5:20
PSC ♓	12/3, 00:00	12/3, 6:20	12/3, 12:30	11/3, 18:30	12/3, 1:00	12/3, 7:00

	1978-79	1979-80	1980-81	1981-82	1982-83	1983-84
PSC ♓	12/3, 7:00	12/3, 13:10	11/3, 19:20	12/3, 1:20	12/3, 7:40	12/3, 13:50
ARI ♈	18/4, 19:10	19/4, 1:20	18/4, 7:20	18/4, 13:40	18/4, 19:50	19/4, 1:50
TAU ♉	14/5, 6:30	14/5, 12:40	13/5, 19:00	14/5, 1:10	14/5, 7:10	14/5, 13:20
GEM ♊	21/6, 14:00	21/6, 20:20	21/6, 2:30	21/6, 8:40	21/6, 14:40	21/6, 20:50
CNC ♋	20/7, 18:50	21/7, 1:10	20/7, 7:20	20/7, 13:30	20/7, 19:30	21/7, 1:40
LEO ♌	10/8, 17:40	11/8, 00:10	10/8, 6:20	10/8, 12:30	10/8, 18:40	11/8, 00:40
VIR ♍	16/9, 19:10	17/9, 1:20	16/9, 7:30	16/9, 13:40	16/9, 19:50	17/9, 2:00
LIB ♎	31/10, 7:20	31/10, 13:30	30/10, 19:40	31/10, 1:50	31/10, 8:00	31/10, 14:20
SCO ♏	23/11, 9:40	23/11, 15:50	22/11, 22:00	23/11, 4:10	23/11, 10:20	23/11, 16:40
OPH Φ	29/11, 22:20	30/11, 4:30	29/11, 10:30	29/11, 16:40	29/11, 22:50	30/11, 5:10
SGR ♐	18/12, 5:50	18/12, 12:00	17/12, 18:00	18/12, 00:10	18/12, 6:20	18/12, 12:30
CAP ♑	20/1, 1:00	20/1, 7:10	19/1, 13:10	19/1, 19:20	20/1, 1:30	20/1, 7:40
AQR ♒	16/2, 11:30	16/2, 17:40	15/2, 23:50	16/2, 6:00	16/2, 12:10	16/2, 18:10
PSC ♓	12/3, 13:10	11/3, 19:20	12/3, 1:20	12/3, 7:40	12/3, 13:50	11/3, 19:40

	1984-85	1985-86	1986-87	1987-88	1988-89	1989-90
PSC ♓	11/3, 19:40	12/3, 2:00	12/3, 8:10	12/3, 14:20	11/3, 20:30	12/3, 2:40
ARI ♈	18/4, 8:00	18/4, 14:10	18/4, 20:10	19/4, 2:20	18/4, 8:30	18/4, 14:50
TAU ♉	13/5, 19:30	14/5, 1:40	14/5, 7:40	14/5, 13:50	13/5, 20:00	14/5, 2:20
GEM ♊	21/6, 3:00	21/6, 9:10	21/6, 15:20	21/6, 21:20	21/6, 3:30	21/6, 9:50
CNC ♋	20/7, 8:00	20/7, 14:00	20/7, 20:10	21/7, 2:10	20/7, 8:20	20/7, 14:40
LEO ♌	10/8, 7:00	10/8, 13:00	10/8, 19:10	11/8, 1:20	10/8, 7:30	10/8, 13:40
VIR ♍	16/9, 8:10	16/9, 14:10	16/9, 20:20	17/9, 2:40	16/9, 8:40	16/9, 14:50
LIB ♎	30/10, 20:20	31/10, 2:30	31/10, 8:40	31/10, 14:50	30/10, 21:00	31/10, 3:10
SCO ♏	22/11, 22:50	23/11, 4:50	23/11, 11:10	23/11, 17:10	22/11, 23:20	23/11, 5:30
OPH Φ	29/11, 11:20	29/11, 17:20	29/11, 23:40	30/11, 5:40	29/11, 11:50	29/11, 18:00
SGR ♐	17/12, 18:50	18/12, 0:50	18/12, 7:00	18/12, 13:10	17/12, 19:10	18/12, 1:30
CAP ♑	19/1, 13:50	19/1, 20:00	20/1, 2:20	20/1, 8:30	19/1, 14:30	19/1, 20:50
AQR ♒	16/2, 00:30	16/2, 6:40	16/2, 12:50	16/2, 19:00	16/2, 1:00	16/2, 7:20
PSC ♓	12/3, 2:00	12/3, 8:10	12/3, 14:20	11/3, 20:30	12/3, 2:40	12/3, 8:50

	1990-91	1991-92	1992-93	1993-94	1994-95	1995-96
PSC ♓	12/3, 8:50	12/3, 15:00	11/3, 21:00	12/3, 3:20	12/3, 9:30	12/3, 15:30
ARI ♈	18/4, 21:00	19/4, 3:00	18/4, 9:10	18/4, 15:30	18/4, 21:30	19/4, 3:40
TAU ♉	14/5, 8:30	14/5, 14:30	13/5, 20:40	14/5, 3:00	14/5, 9:00	14/5, 15:00
GEM ♊	21/6, 15:50	21/6, 22:00	21/6, 4:20	21/6, 10:20	21/6, 16:30	21/6, 22:40
CNC ♋	20/7, 20:40	21/7, 2:50	20/7, 9:10	20/7, 15:10	20/7, 21:20	21/7, 3:30
LEO ♌	10/8, 19:40	11/8, 1:50	10/8, 8:10	10/8, 14:20	10/8, 20:20	11/8, 2:30
VIR ♍	16/9, 20:50	17/9, 3:00	16/9, 9:20	16/9, 15:20	16/9, 21:30	17/9, 3:50
LIB ♎	31/10, 9:10	31/10, 15:20	30/10, 21:30	31/10, 3:40	31/10, 9:50	31/10, 16:00
SCO ♏	23/11, 11:40	23/11, 17:50	23/11, 00:00	23/11, 6:00	23/11, 12:20	23/11, 18:40
OPH Φ	30/11, 00:10	30/11, 6:20	29/11, 12:20	29/11, 18:30	30/11, 00:40	30/11, 6:50
SGR ♐	18/12, 7:40	18/12, 13:40	17/12, 20:00	18/12, 2:00	18/12, 8:10	18/12, 14:30
CAP ♑	20/1, 2:50	20/1, 9:00	19/1, 15:10	19/1, 21:10	20/1, 3:30	20/1, 9:40
AQR ♒	16/2, 13:30	16/2, 19:30	16/2, 1:50	16/2, 7:50	16/2, 14:00	16/2, 20:10
PSC ♓	12/3, 15:00	11/3, 21:00	12/3, 3:20	12/3, 9:30	12/3, 15:30	11/3, 21:40

	1996-97	1997-98	1998-99	1999-2000	2000-01	2001-02
PSC ♓	11/3, 21:40	12/3, 3:50	12/3, 10:00	12/3, 16:20	11/3, 22:20	12/3, 4:40
ARI ♈	18/4, 9:40	18/4, 15:50	18/4, 22:10	19/4, 4:20	18/4, 10:30	18/4, 16:40
TAU ♉	13/5, 21:20	14/5, 3:20	14/5, 9:30	14/5, 15:40	13/5, 21:50	14/5, 4:10
GEM ♊	21/6, 4:50	21/6, 11:00	21/6, 17:00	21/6, 23:10	21/6, 5:30	21/6, 11:40
CNC ♋	20/7, 9:40	20/7, 15:50	20/7, 21:50	21/7, 4:00	20/7, 10:20	20/7, 16:20
LEO ♌	10/8, 8:50	10/8, 14:50	10/8, 21:00	11/8, 3:10	10/8, 9:20	10/8, 15:30
VIR ♍	16/9, 10:00	16/9, 16:10	16/9, 22:20	17/9, 4:20	16/9, 10:40	16/9, 16:40
LIB ♎	30/10, 22:10	31/10, 4:20	31/10, 10:30	31/10, 16:40	30/10, 22:50	31/10, 4:50
SCO ♏	23/11, 00:40	23/11, 7:00	23/11, 13:00	23/11, 19:10	23/11, 1:30	23/11, 7:30
OPH Φ	29/11, 13:10	29/11, 19:20	30/11, 1:20	30/11, 7:30	29/11, 13:40	29/11, 19:50
SGR ♐	17/12, 20:30	18/12, 2:50	18/12, 9:00	18,12, 15:00	17/12, 21:10	18/12, 3:20
CAP ♑	19/1, 15:40	19/1, 22:00	20/1, 4:10	20/1, 10:20	19/1, 16:30	19/1, 22:30
AQR ♒	16/2, 2:10	16/2, 8:30	16/2, 14:50	16/2, 20:50	16/2, 3:00	16/2, 9:10
PSC ♓	12/3, 3:50	12/3, 10:00	12/3, 16:20	11/3, 22:20	12/3, 4:40	12/3, 10:50

	2002-03	2003-04	2004-05	2005-06	2006-07	2007-08
PSC ♓	12/3, 10:50	12/3, 16:40	11/3, 23:00	12/3, 5:10	12/3, 11:20	12/3, 17:30
ARI ♈	18/4, 22:50	19/4, 4:50	18/4, 11:00	18/4, 17:10	18/4, 23:20	19/4, 5:30
TAU ♉	14/5, 10:20	14/5, 16:20	13/5, 22:30	14/5, 4:40	14/5, 10:50	14/5, 17:00
GEM ♊	21/6, 17:50	21/6, 23:50	21/6, 6:00	21/6, 12:20	21/6, 18:20	22/6, 00:20
CNC ♋	20/7, 22:30	21/7, 4:40	20/7, 10:50	20/7, 17:00	20/7, 23:10	21/7, 5:10
LEO ♌	10/8, 21:30	11/8, 3:40	10/8, 10:00	10/8, 16:10	10/8, 22:10	11/8, 4:20
VIR ♍	16/9, 22:40	17/9, 5:00	16/9, 11:10	16/9, 17:20	16/9, 23:30	17/9, 5:30
LIB ♎	31/10, 11:00	31/10, 17:10	30/10, 23:20	31/10, 5:30	31/10, 11:40	31/10, 17:50
SCO ♏	23/11, 13:40	23/11, 19:50	23/11, 2:00	23/11, 8:10	23/11, 14:20	23/11, 20:30
OPH Φ	30/11, 2:00	30/11, 8:10	29/11, 14:10	29/11, 20:20	30/11, 2:30	30/11, 8:50
SGR ♐	18/12, 9:30	18/12, 15:40	17/12, 21:40	18/12, 3:50	18/12, 10:10	18/12, 16:10
CAP ♑	20/1, 4:50	20/1, 11:00	19/1, 17:00	19/1, 23:00	20/1, 5:20	20/1, 11:20
AQR ♒	16/2, 15:20	16/2, 21:30	16/2, 3:30	16/2, 9:50	16/2, 15:50	16/2, 21:50
PSC ♓	12/3, 16:40	11/3, 23:00	12/3, 5:10	12/3, 11:20	12/3, 17:30	11/3, 23:30

	2008-09	2009-10	2010-11	2011-12	2012-13	2013-14
PSC ♓	11/3, 23:30	12/3, 5:40	12/3, 12:00	12/3, 18:00	12/3, 00:20	12/3, 6:20
ARI ♈	18/4, 11:30	18/4, 17:50	19/4, 00:00	19/4, 6:00	18/4, 12:20	18/4, 18:30
TAU ♉	13/5, 23:00	14/5, 5:20	14/5, 11:20	14/5, 17:30	13/5, 23:50	14/5, 6:00
GEM ♊	21/6, 6:40	21/6, 12:50	21/6, 18:50	22/6, 1:00	21/6, 7:10	21/6, 13:20
CNC ♋	20/7, 11:30	20/7, 17:30	20/7, 23:40	21/7, 5:50	20/7, 12:00	20/7, 18:10
LEO ♌	10/8, 10:30	10/8, 16:40	10/8, 22:50	11/8, 4:50	10/8, 11:10	10/8, 17:20
VIR ♍	16/9, 11:40	16/9, 17:50	16/9, 23:50	17/9, 6:10	16/9, 12:20	16/9, 18:30
LIB ♎	31/10, 00:00	31/10, 6:00	31/10, 12:20	31/10, 18:30	31/10, 00:40	31/10, 6:50
SCO ♏	23/11, 2:50	23/11, 8:50	23/11, 15:00	23/11, 21:20	23/11, 3:20	23/11, 9:30
OPH Φ	29/11, 15:00	29/11, 21:00	30/11, 3:20	30/11, 9:20	29/11, 15:30	29/11, 21:40
SGR ♐	17/12, 22:30	18/12, 4:30	18/12, 10:40	18/12, 17:00	17/12, 23:00	18/12, 5:10
CAP ♑	19/1, 17:40	19/1, 23:50	20/1, 6:00	20/1, 12:10	19/1, 18:10	20/1, 00:20
AQR ♒	16/2, 4:10	16/2, 10:30	16/2, 16:30	16/2, 22:50	16/2, 4:50	16/2, 11:00
PSC ♓	12/3, 5:40	12/3, 12:00	12/3, 18:00	12/3, 00:20	12/3, 6:20	12/3, 12:30

	2014-15	2015-16	2016-17	2017-18	2018-19	2019-20
PSC ♓	12/3, 12:30	12/3, 18:50	12/3, 00:50	12/3, 7:00	12/3, 13:10	12/3, 19:10
ARI ♈	19/4, 00:40	19/4, 6:50	18/4, 12:50	18/4, 19:10	19/4, 1:10	19/4, 7:10
TAU ♉	14/5, 12:00	14/5, 18:10	14/5, 00:20	14/5, 6:30	14/5, 12:40	14/5, 18:40
GEM ♊	21/6, 19:40	22/6, 1:40	21/6, 8:00	21/6, 14:00	21/6, 20:10	22/6, 2:10
CNC ♋	21/7, 00:20	21/7, 6:30	20/7, 12:50	20/7, 18:50	21/7, 1:00	21/7, 7:10
LEO ♌	10/8, 23:20	11/8, 5:40	10/8, 11:50	10/8, 18:00	11/8, 00:00	11/8, 6:10
VIR ♍	17/9, 00:40	17/9, 6:40	16/9, 13:00	16/9, 19:10	17/9, 1:10	17/9, 7:30
LIB ♎	31/10, 12:50	31/10, 19:00	31/10, 1:10	31/10, 7:20	31/10, 13:30	31/10, 19:40
SCO ♏	23/11, 15:40	23/11, 21:50	23/11, 4:10	23/11, 10:10	23/11, 16:20	23/11, 22:40
OPH Φ	30/11, 3:50	30/11, 10:00	29/11, 16:10	29/11, 22:10	30/11, 4:30	30/11, 10:40
SGR ♐	18/12, 11:30	18/12, 17:20	17/12, 23:40	18/12, 5:40	18/12, 11:50	18/12, 18:10
CAP ♑	20/1, 6:40	20/1, 12:40	19/1, 19:00	20/1, 1:00	20/1, 7:10	20/1, 13:20
AQR ♒	16/2, 17:10	16/2, 23:10	16/2, 5:30	16/2, 11:40	16/2, 17:40	16/2, 23:50
PSC ♓	12/3, 18:50	12/3, 0:50	12/3, 7:00	12/3, 13:10	12/3, 19:10	12/3, 1:20

About the Author

Vasilis Kanatas was born in Amfissa, in the Municipality of Delphi. He is a physicist and wrote his dissertation entitled: "Concerning Constellations" in the fields of Astronomy & Uranography. In this work he described the 88 constellations of the sky and came in contact with Horoscopic Astrology and the 13 Zodiac Constellations.
He is an amateur astronomer and member of the Amateur Astronomy Association "Achyrostrata" (named after an ancient word for our galaxy used by local people), based in the Municipality of Delphi. In the meetings of the club, he makes presentations on scientific topics and issues of Uranography.
He is also interested in Cosmology.

Printed in Great Britain
by Amazon

62525357R00108